What They Say about "Design for Identity"

"Empathy and understanding are core principles of user centered design. Yet we seem to struggle as a society to understand the impact of race, gender identity, and culture outside of our own lived experiences. Grounded in concrete examples ranging from innocent mistakes to willful ignorance, students, interior designers and architects will learn from the mistakes of others and Bantom's wisdom as they strive to center the cultural identity of all users in their designed solutions. This book should be required reading in every architecture and design program."

> **Doug Seidler,** Director, School of Design + Art and Professor, Interior Design at Marymount University

"In our unique way, each of us has a hand in designing a more equitable world. We design every day, but without close attention to who's included, heard, and valued as an integral part of that process, we will be designing an incomplete future. Jessica has laid out a roadmap for all designers that invites us to consider how we might shift our process to generate a more complete and representative reality. This book is a critical contribution to the conversation."

> **Jennifer Brown,** Founder and CEO, Jennifer Brown Consulting, Best-Selling Author of *Inclusion, Beyond Diversity* and *How to Be an Inclusive Leader*

"Inequality in all of its forms is just as much a threat to our future and our present as are the issues of our environment's care and our sustainability concerns. The fact that higher density cities are going to be the norm due to the need for resiliency and that we are all going to be living and working together in closer proximity, architects and designers of all backgrounds and cultures are going to be needed as the mediators in our cultural differences to bring us together in peaceful coexistence. If events in our country and society at large continues on the track that it has since the end of slavery, the dawn of Civil Rights and Reconstruction after the Civil War, then in my opinion, the turmoil we went through these past few years will seem like a cocktail party in comparison to what will happen in the future when the cities and environments we design and live in are even more densely and diversely populated. The fact that most of the world's population will be living in urban centers has been projected by economists, think tanks and policy makers as we are witnessing across the country and globally in the next fifty years.

In Jessica Bantom's beautifully articulated thesis and book, *Design for Identity*, our epoch needs to come to an understanding that we need to be prepared to deal with the culturally sensitive matters of what we design and how it is that we design in the service of an increasingly diverse and urban focused population. Jessica's book and its advice is timely and perhaps overdue. I hope that it will be valued in design theory classes throughout all design programs in universities as a standard must read and in our profession as architects, planners and designers."

Michael Marshall, FAIA NOMA NCARB

"I met Jessica when she was a standout facilitator for an organization I was partnering with. Jessica did not call herself a standout, she just listened better and made connections better than a significant majority of others in the culture and diversity-to-belonging spaces. It was for this reason that I knew she would make a good author. It's not easy to truly help people help themselves explore, understand, and resolve their longstanding biases and knowledge gaps, but Jessica's ability to take on complex, often subjective, and always emotional topics made it easy. I read her book and automatically wondered why she is not in a college classroom helping students conceptualize and master the criticality of equity and belonging. These are not academic topics. They require dialogue that is often avoided today. Jessica's book is this conversation starter, not only for the content but because of the inviting and challenging nature of how she writes. This is what stands out to me about her and her book, which I will be recommending to anyone and everyone who wants to understand the diversity, equity, inclusion, and belonging spectrum."

Chris Armstrong, Certified Master Facilitator, Certified Diversity Executive

"Jessica's writing style makes a critical concept accessible to those in the profession and all humans, highlighting the critical nature of cultural competence onto all of life's processes, not just design."

Leslie Traub, Partner, Udarta Consulting

"*Design for Identity* is a must-read for forward-thinking designers willing to design beyond the competitive edge! The book takes the mystery out of applying cultural awareness to the existing design process. It will inspire your creativity and change your approach to problem solving."

Towanna Burrous, Founder and President, CoachDiversity Institute

"Jessica brings years of experience in intentional design thinking and takes the conversation about human-centered design to the next level. *Design for Identity* not only asks us to explore our personal role in designing culturally competent solutions, but it asks organizations to transform their own cultures to create inclusive and empathetic solutions for their diverse customers. The book is what creative problem solvers have been waiting for!"

Maia Sciupac, Innovation Lead & Experience Designer at Booz Allen Hamilton

"*Design for Identity* is essential reading for any business that truly wants to roll out the welcome mat! Jessica Bantom weaves together fresh design ideas, unexpected evidence, and compelling stories empowering you to inclusively design by centering those of us who are often left out of the conversation. Each page of this powerful book offers doses of inspiration and an enhanced sense of what is possible when it comes to thinking about the future of work. Do yourself a favor and pick up a copy and begin taking those actions that are within reach today!"

Rhodes Perry, CEO, Rhodes Perry Consulting, Best-Selling Author of *Belonging at Work* and *Imagine Belonging*

"The time for business leaders, creative problem solvers, and community to come together to enhance and shape our everyday experiences couldn't be more ripe. I'm excited and thrilled about what practitioners, doers, and thought leaders in design alike are going to come away from not only reading Jessica's book, but what they will learn from her wisdom, creative spirit, and natural ability to see the best in all of us. She has a knack for finding ways to help individuals from disparate teams work together to make something not only pleasing to the eye, but more importantly starting with being equitable too."

Gabriel Arteaga, CoFounder and CEO, Create&

"Symbols hold meaning but without awareness of a textured context, designers of homes, workplaces, and interactions can create dissonance and alienate rather than engage and include. Jessica Bantom's *Design for Identity* is a welcome perspective on how to become more sensitized to context, diverse perceptions of reality and a stronger capacity to detect nuance that is characteristic of complex environments.

Bringing her rejuvenating energy to the page, Jessica breaks down into simple opportunities offering every designer or decision maker a chance to be clear and mindful about intent and purpose, with a focus on positive impact. Being human is not easy and *Design for Identity* brings compassion and profound simplicity to moving away from a one-dimensional view toward a multi-perspective way of benefiting from the unique aspect of every person's identity. By embedding greater attention to what designers pay attention to, Jessica's book draws attention to what designers focus on. Unconscious habits, application of design lenses, and elevating the scope of the thinking or purpose each offer entry into uplifting conscious competence.

At a time when decisions have overlooked ways to be better at being human, more than designers can benefit from the insights that are relevant to every person regardless of how they identify."

Dawna Jones, Organizational and Decision Ecologist

"*Design for Identity* is a groundbreaking book on the cultural transformation of design theory and practice by incorporating the experiences of traditionally marginalized communities including Black people and People of Color. Drawing on trenchant examples from her work experience, case studies, as well interviews with practitioners and teachers, Jessica Bantom shows what designing for cultural competency means and how it can be taught and practiced in the industry today."

Melissa Fisher Ph.D., Cultural Anthropologist, Author of *Wall Street Women*, New York University Institute for Public Knowledge and School of Professional Studies

"Jessica's book is a super relevant and significant contribution to the zeitgeist as companies and individuals seek to design a more inclusive and innovative world!"

Natalie Nixon, PhD, Author of *The Creativity Leap: Unleash Curiosity, Improvisation and Intuition at Work*

"To design for inclusivity without excluding or alienating is what Jessica applies throughout her pages. She understands how the space we occupy at any given moment can have such different impacts on the individual and how that impact influences performance, mood, and a sense of belonging. She allows us to design through multiple lenses, to be human-centric to a diverse population.

The need to design for belonging is not limited to designers. I have incorporated some of the ideas to meetings, documents, and other daily business activities.

Design for Identity is a powerful read for anyone wanting to create an inclusive environment and a must read for design professionals."

B Greenberg, Founder, Changeship

How to Design Authentically
for a Diverse World

JESSICA BANTOM

Foreword by Leatrice Eiseman, Director of the
Eiseman Center for Color Information & Training and
Executive Director of the Pantone® Color Institute

Afterword by Kia Weatherspoon, CID, NCIDQ, ASID,
D.F.A (h.c), Founder + President of Determined by Design

For permission requests, write to the publisher, addressed "Attention: Permissions Coordinator," at the address below.

Publish Your Purpose
141 Weston Street, #155
Hartford, CT, 06141

The opinions expressed by the Author are not necessarily those held by Publish Your Purpose.

Ordering Information: Quantity sales and special discounts are available on quantity purchases by corporations, associations, and others. For details, contact the publisher at hello@publishyourpurpose.com.

Edited by: August Li, Kassandra White
Author Photo Credit: Delores Holloway, a little bit of whimsy photography
Cover design by: Designerbility
Typeset by: Nelly Murariu

Printed in the United States of America.
ISBN: 979-8-88797-014-1 (hardcover)
ISBN: 979-8-88797-013-4 (paperback)
ISBN: 979-8-88797-015-8 (ebook)

Library of Congress Control Number: 2022921978

First edition, April 2023.

Publish Your Purpose is a hybrid publisher of non-fiction books. Our mission is to elevate the voices often excluded from traditional publishing. We intentionally seek out authors and storytellers with diverse backgrounds, life experiences, and unique perspectives to publish books that will make an impact in the world. Do you have a book idea you would like us to consider publishing? Please visit PublishYourPurpose.com for more information.

DEDICATION

To 1511 –

You made me.

We made it.

TO THE READERS

If you react to this book with doubt,
disbelief, or anger, ask yourself why.

I implore you to read it again and
consider discussing it with other people.

You are my most intended audience.

CONTENTS

FOREWORD

by Leatrice Eiseman

I n one of my books, *Pantone Guide to Communicating With Color*, I referred to color as a "silent salesperson." Even without the use of verbiage, color is known to work synergistically with all of the senses, symbolizes abstract concepts and thoughts, expresses fantasy and wish-fulfillment, recalls another time or place, and produces an esthetic or emotional response.

As research and experience inform us, from clothing and cosmetics to cars and carpets, color is the magical ingredient for clinching the sale and the most effective means of delivering a message without saying a word. From the moment you enter a space, you are inundated with the sense of the colors surrounding you. It is the first thing you notice when you enter and the final message that you take away when you leave.

Color is a critical element of design, which overall has the magnified power to communicate messages, either bringing people down or lifting them up, pushing people away or drawing them in. *Design for Identity* teaches us how to harness the power of design, so we can be good, responsible stewards.

When I taught Jessica at the Eiseman Center for Color Information and Training, I knew I had encountered a designer who was poised to make powerful connections that would push us all to see the world from a different perspective. Her background in both business and design gave her practical and artistic sensibilities that inform her holistic approach to solving for very real human challenges.

This book is a testament to her vision. She speaks to the designer from a relatable place of sincere care for the practice, the art, and the customer — a place that resonates with me because I know that combination has to come from the heart. It is the artist in us that wants to add beauty to the world and the subject matter expert who wants that beauty to also serve a purpose.

Now is the perfect time for *Design for Identity*. In this time when we're navigating a pandemic-induced heightened awareness of difference, an expanding interconnected global economy, and new expectations from younger generations, our dialogue must evolve. Jessica lays out a path for us to get there.

In her words, start where you are, and we can all do our part to make design — and our world — more inclusive.

Teatrice Eiseman,

Director of the Eiseman Center for Color Information & Training, Executive Director of the Pantone® Color Institute

INTRODUCTION

June 2022 marked the first nationwide commercial observance of Juneteenth, a remembrance previously celebrated among Black Americans acknowledging the official emancipation of the last known enslaved people in 1865. For me, the new Juneteenth products I saw online and on store shelves reaffirmed why I wrote this book. In the very typical response of our capitalist culture, a day of historical significance was reduced to a Great Value ice-cream flavor and tone-deaf party favors with appropriated sayings like "It's the freedom for me" sold by Walmart. The disgust I felt was only surpassed by my amazement that in this day and age, design teams somewhere collaborated to come up with the packaging for that dessert and the layout for those can coolers. Who was or was not in the room when those tone-deaf decisions were being made?

This experience took me back to my days as an interior design student. At that point, I had four years of professional experience in consulting and marketing. I was used to being "the only" or one of few who looked like me in work settings. But nowhere else did the significance of that reality strike me the way it did in design. I was being taught about the importance of form and function, as well as centering the customer in the design process. However, as I navigated design studios, industry events, and professional settings filled with white students, instructors, and practitioners, it became clear that the customer we were designing for was not me. In fact, it couldn't be any customer from a marginalized group because identity was rarely a part of the design dialogue. A very serious question occurred to me: If designers design for everyone, how can there be so little diversity in the profession?

I found it troubling to think a profession that did not intentionally address topics of race, ethnicity, religion, socioeconomic status, or sexual identity, for example, was responsible for designing spaces that accommodate people who identify differently in all of these ways. I found it even more troubling to think that designers didn't even seem to find identity worthy of discussion, either because they didn't care or because they thought they had all these nuances figured out themselves without the input of the people of different backgrounds. I also found myself wondering what hope the small number of designers like me had of injecting our voices to inform the design of the world being shaped around us.

All these thoughts led me to write this book. I wanted to explore these disconnects that have characterized the interior design profession, and design overall, as I've known it. I wanted to draw attention to this chasm that has endured despite affirmative action; diversity, equity, and inclusion efforts; federal mandates; begrudging policy changes; corporate statements; and pledges of allyship. I wanted to explore the implications of designing anything from spaces to products to fashion and images based only on research, focus groups, or assumptions. I wanted to explore how we could do things differently, so different perspectives are factored into the design process and not just taken into consideration due to fallout after public backlash.

To give you a little insight into what has shaped my perspectives, I'll start from the beginning. I'm a Black female born and raised in Philadelphia and the daughter of a former interior designer. Because that was my reality, design didn't seem inconceivable as a career path. However, due to the volatility of the market of the eighties, which forced my mother out of the profession, I had my doubts about the stability of design as a career choice. Fast forward several years, an undergraduate degree in English, a job in marketing, and a transition to IT consulting later, I realized my passion was worth pursuing, and I enrolled to get my master's in interior design.

Having attended a predominantly white university and with a few years of professional experience under my belt, I wasn't surprised that there were very few people who looked like me in my classes and none at the front of the room. There were, however, many international students in my program. Somewhere in the back of my naïve mind, I thought maybe I'd learn about how people used space in different cultures as we developed and shared our projects during endless peer reviews and concept development discussions.

I was wrong.

When we got a project to redesign a church into a community center, I thought surely we would get into some juicy conversations. What denomination was the church? What was the makeup of the surrounding community? What would possibly be considered sacred in the space and so should remain untouched or at least treated with care? What would be an acceptable and meaningful way to repurpose a facility like that? Having been raised in a Baptist church and in an area that would have greatly benefited from a community center, I felt sure we would explore the many perspectives to be considered in such a project. And once again, I was wrong. It became a rote exercise about form and function, not people.

This became a pattern throughout my education. Surprisingly, it was even the case when we talked about residential design, by far one of the most personal areas of specialty as it involves how people function in their private domain. There was no consideration of the many factors that impact people's existence — their ethnic customs (multigenerational households), religious background (space for prayer or an altar, kosher food storage), or their generational beliefs (a preference for more closed-off or private spaces), to name a few. And despite there being as many different upbringings as there were students in the class, there was no space given to explore and learn from one another to equip us to be truly dynamic, engaging, and thoughtful designers.

Not being one to confine my education to a classroom, I explored various industry associations, events, and settings. Having had some exposure to the "real world," I was curious to see if things were any different elsewhere. If I thought I stood out at school, I was really in for some eye-opening moments at association meetings. Or in design center show-rooms. Or at conferences or continuing education workshops. Once again, I was way outnumbered, and once again, none of the topics we discussed got into the ways people live, what they value, or what they identify with. The only major areas of difference discussed concerned designing for people with differing abilities and for aging populations — definitely considerations that merit great attention, but even they seemed largely tied to ADA, compliance, and codes. Back to form and function, not people.

And then I stumbled into my sweet spot. I had always been curious about color, and I anticipated learning — either in the classroom or through industry — about its physiolog-ical and biological effects, its symbolism, and its meanings. In my mind, it was such a dynamic topic surely it would be discussed somewhere. It was but I had to search for it — and it was all the way across the country in San Diego.

After some pretty extensive research, I found the Internatio-nal Association of Color Consultants—North America (IACCNA).

They were the only organization I could find that taught color to the in-depth level I was seeking. And that series of seminars I participated in during my last couple semesters of my degree program was the first time in my design education that I learned design philosophies from different cultures and the meanings of color in different belief systems. I engaged with and learned from people in a space where they freely spoke about design from their own background and experience. That was it. That was what I was looking for!

But I came to see that experience was an anomaly, one I attribute to the fact that the IACCNA is rooted in an international organization. I finished out my program and entered the design industry, where I wouldn't encounter that open dialogue or expression again unless I made space for it.

It was — and is — soul-crushing to me that the interior design industry has not come that far in the fifteen years I've been a part of it. I'm still meeting Black designers who are the only one in their firms of one hundred-plus people. In such an environment, how and where can people of underrepresented groups find and use their voices? And if they can't, on what basis are the other designers designing — for them and everyone else?

The interior design industry isn't the only space where this is an issue. Through my work in marketing, I've engaged frequently with the graphic design industry. And through my exploration and education in design thinking as well as my IT consulting experience, I've had significant exposure to the product design industry and UI/UX design. The lack of representation is very real there as well.

Now, as an IT turned management turned Diversity, Equity, Inclusion & Belonging consultant who has simultaneously engaged in multiple facets of design, I come back to my original question: If designers design for everyone, how can there be so little diversity in the profession? I hope you'll take this journey with me to explore the significance of this question and to make the changes, both individually and collectively, to ensure everyone sees more of themselves in what designers design.

The mission of this book is to influence current and future generations of designers to bring their own voices and to invite others' voices into the design process for outcomes that reflect the breadth of humanity. This applies to all designers, regardless of discipline — interior designers, graphic designers, product designers, fashion designers — anyone who plans the form or structure of something before it is made, as the term designer is defined. That definition alone makes it clear why this book is relevant. We, as designers, are the creators of concepts and the originators of the stuff that helps shape people's existence. Because we are instrumental in the form-ing of things, it is on us to specify what goes into the process. And what is something crafted for humanity if recognition of humanity is left out of its creation?

For practicing designers, this book is a call to reevaluate your design process. It provides insights to factor into your thought processes, your planning, and your interaction with clients, customers, end users, and colleagues to ensure you approach your practice from an informed standpoint and not one based on assumptions and personal interpretations of what people consider significant.

For future designers, this book is a foundation for forming your design philosophy and practice. It is meant to expand your appreciation for the scope of the duty of designers and to introduce perspectives into the process that are not typically incorporated in design education. It presents an opportunity for you to design your approach to design in a way that introduces bold and necessary dialogue to systematically revolutionize and humanize long-standing processes. It gives you what you need to adapt your craft to shine a light on unseen populations and bring about outcomes that reflect an ever-evolving world.

It is my intention to provoke thought and conversation and, ultimately, a shift in our practice of design. So let's get into the significance of designing with cultural competence, and then we'll explore the blueprint for the practice itself.

1

CULTURAL COMPETENCE FOR DESIGN FIRMS

I n late 2021, I caught up with a colleague who worked as a designer in a huge global firm. We were talking about the aftermath of the summer of 2020 when the murder of George Floyd by police officers fueled what seemed to be an impassioned call for racial justice, even from corporations that never spoke to the topic previously in a public forum. As we discussed subsequent changes in our own organizations, I was dismayed by what she told me.

Her firm proudly promotes diversity and inclusion. Its website has a whole page dedicated to statements of commitment, information about employee resource groups, and diversity and inclusion awards they've won. But when it came down to it, the only shift she had seen in the execution of design work post-2020 was a call to use images of people of diverse backgrounds in their renderings. Clearly, something about honoring identity in a significant way wasn't translating between corporate philosophy and delivery of design services.

What Is Cultural Competence?

For various reasons, including the social justice shift we experienced following the murder of George Floyd, today's social climate requires organizations to take stock of their consciousness of cultural issues (the "what") and the ways they operate based on that awareness (the "how"). Collectively, I refer to this as their Culture Quotient. It is a combination of their cultural awareness (acknowledgement of similarities and differences among cultural groups) and their cultural competence (the ability to understand, appreciate, and interact with people from cultures or belief systems different from their own.)

FIGURE 1—CULTURE QUOTIENT

Cultural awareness is acquired through standard knowledge-building means, such as training and workshops. It's rooted in learning the concepts, terminology, and conduct related to cultural difference and operating in culturally diverse spaces. In short, it's about learning theory. But when we pivot to cultural competence, we put all that theory into practice. Cultural competence is about action. It requires translating knowledge about cultural difference into new behaviors, practices, and viewpoints and doing our jobs and engaging with people in ways that signify respect for the different ways they exist according to their varied backgrounds, experiences, and traits.

Cultural awareness would be adding religious observances to your corporate calendar beyond those tied to Christian traditions and holidays. Cultural competence would be having a discussion with your workforce about the daily routine changes required to properly commemorate those observances and how they can be accommodated in the workplace. One is about acknowledging difference and the other is about acting with respect for the difference. The combination is what's most impactful but cultural competence is the game changer. Many of us get to the awareness and think our work is done but cultural competence is what's necessary to bring about different outcomes for people who have been historically excluded — in our firms, in our industries, and in society.

When it comes down to it, cultural competence is the ultimate desired outcome of all the diversity, equity, inclusion, and belonging (DEIB) work being done across organizations today.

Because DEIB forms the basis for the discussion of cultural competence in this text, let's back up a little to cover some basics. As this practice area has evolved, it has been referred to by many terms and acronyms. In the era of affirmative action, diversity was the main focus. The emphasis was on opening doors and increasing numbers of people in underrepresented or, at that time, non-represented groups. As it became clear that opening doors did not equate to people wanting to stay within those doors, the discussion expanded to introduce inclusion. Being included did not equate to being treated fairly, so equity became a part of the conversation. And following all this emphasis on what was being done *for* people, belonging came into play to gauge *whether and how* those people perceived and received any resulting differences in their experiences and outcomes. (Note: This field of practice also incorporates Justice (DEIJ, JEDI) and Accessibility (DEIA, IDEA) in some spaces, and the order and priority of terms may also vary (EDI). Terminology will no doubt continue to evolve as the subject, its treatment, and the dialogue evolves.)

Here's how each term is defined:

1. **Diversity** means realistic representation among stakeholders, both internal and external — representation that mirrors the makeup of our society.

2. **Equity** means fair treatment and access to opportunity, reward, safety, and security.

3. **Inclusion** means inviting people to show up as their true selves and valuing the contributions they make as a result.

4. **Belonging** refers to how well acts of inclusion resonate with individuals and how much they feel like they have a place in an organization.

DEIB is not just a practice area. DEIB is also not a project or initiative, as it is often treated and referred to in organizations. Diversity, equity, inclusion, and belonging are a set of values. DEIB work is about helping individuals and organizations develop an understanding of those values and shift their mindsets, so they can relate and work effectively in culturally diverse situations based on cultural awareness and embed those values into how they operate and show up in the world (i.e., act with cultural competence). (Note: As a frame of reference, this book addresses culture, diversity, and difference based on several dimensions of humanity, including race, ethnicity, gender, sexual orientation, age, class, ability, and religion.)

For an organization, the scope of DEIB work ranges from the internal to the external and from the individual throughout the entire organization. As illustrated in the DEIB Value Continuum shown below, it is critical to center DEIB within the organization's culture. By doing so, those values permeate across all levels and departments. This internal alignment then positions the organization to live those values outwardly, with authenticity and consistency in all of its external stakeholder relationships and, ultimately, in society.

So why is all this important specifically in the context of design? As designers, you design for everyone. Even if you are commissioned to design a space or an object for one particular client, you have no control over who else will possess or experience that space or object out in the world. Therefore, it is your duty to approach your work as though you are designing for all humankind.

Is that a tall order? Yes.

Will you ever please or satisfy absolutely everyone who encounters what you design? No.

But the point is to approach your work as a service to people of diverse backgrounds, experiences, capabilities, perspectives, beliefs, and practices. And to honor those facets in all the people who are a part of the design process with you. Going back to the meaning of cultural competence, this requires you to have the capacity to understand, appreciate, and interact with people from cultures or belief systems different from your own.

FIGURE 2—DEIB VALUE CONTINUUM

ORGANIZATION

LEADERSHIP

DIVISION

MANAGER

TEAM

INDIVIDUAL

Cultural Competence

Diversity, Equity, Inclusion & Belonging as Lived Values

CULTURE

WORKFORCE

CUSTOMERS

SUPPLIERS + PARTNERS

INDUSTRY

SOCIETY

The Importance of Cultural Competence for a Design Firm

As the DEIB Value Continuum illustrates, centering and living the values of diversity, equity, inclusion, and belonging are critical to operating with cultural competence from the individual level up through the organizational level and from within an organization outwards. But what are the specific outcomes of operating with cultural competence for a design firm?

When your design firm embeds these values and functions in a way that reflects and honors difference in people, it creates opportunities for a different kind of dialogue. It creates an environment where you acknowledge different practices, motivations, and needs among your workforce and your network of business partners and vendors. It enables an environment where connections can be drawn between your work and our ever-evolving society, with its shifting demographics and the impacts those shifts will have on what and how you create. It fosters an environment where difference isn't a scary topic to be avoided but one that reveals opportunities to think and function on a level that can position you to tap into unexplored resources and adapt to survive and thrive.

Scan this QR code
to download the
DEIB Value Continuum.

Benefits of Cultural Competence

Bottom line, cultural competence broadens your firm's scope of human experience on a macro level and positions you to act more strategically over the long term. Here are just a few of the benefits that creates.

FIGURE 3—BENEFITS OF CULTURAL COMPETENCE

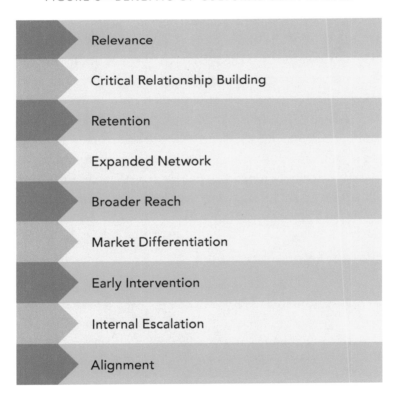

Relevance

Critical Relationship Building

Retention

Expanded Network

Broader Reach

Market Differentiation

Early Intervention

Internal Escalation

Alignment

Relevance

> Remaining relevant in our increasingly global economy requires responding to societal and generational demands for increased accountability around DEIB, which is facilitated through cultural competence.

We are living in a pivotal time when values are shifting among society and generations. Diversity, equity, inclusion, belonging, and the acceptance of difference are no longer concepts reserved for the HR department. The floodgates have opened; corporate statements have been made, and your future talent pool, your customers, your partners, and your industry are looking for changes to be made because the times demand it. The mindset shift has been slow coming, but it will not go backwards. Firms that embrace and strive for cultural competence will be the ones that can meet this demand and remain significant as the dialogue continues to evolve on a global scale.

Critical Relationship Building

> The knowledge and appreciation of difference inherent in cultural competence equips individuals and businesses to communicate more effectively and in more meaningful ways with colleagues and customers.

From a business standpoint, it is critical to always be on the lookout for untapped markets and unserved needs. A firm that broadens its understanding of different cultures and belief systems is more likely to be successful in that search. And a firm that can proactively engage and connect with the people in those markets, because they've taken the time to understand them, is going to be that much further ahead.

To take it a step further, a firm with a more diverse workforce is going to have an inside track to gain insight into those markets because they'll have the knowledge in-house. And with the people come the connections that can broaden your talent pool, your professional network, your perspectives, and your understanding of ways your product can be transformed to sell. Furthermore, that appreciation of difference among your workforce emboldens people to share ideas and engage in ways that bubble up innovation.

Retention

> Employees and customers stay where they feel seen and where their experience and identity are acknowledged through culturally competent engagement.

If they feel that their experience and identity are not only seen but *valued*, they will not have to be convinced or feel resigned to stay aligned with you. They will want to. From a business perspective, it costs a lot more to hire an employee or reel in a new customer than it does to retain the ones you have. Why not invest the time to understand them better to keep them? Are there unexplored facets of your customer's lifestyle that could strengthen their loyalty to your clothing line? Is your firm equipped to pivot and show clients how to repurpose spaces based on shifts in the surrounding demographics? As an employer, are you ready to ask questions that uncover perspectives from your staff's lived experience that will help positively evolve their work experience in terms of policy, practice, and workplace code of conduct? These are indicators of cultural competence that will touch hearts and minds and resonate with people in ways that create meaningful, sustainable relationships.

BOOST YOUR
CULTURE QUOTIENT

Lived experience is defined as first-hand experience living as a member of a historically excluded group. It is a broad term that encapsulates the inequities, challenges, microaggressions, and other nuances people in marginalized groups experience in various contexts and settings.

Expanded Network

> Increased cultural competence opens doors to expanding your reach beyond what's familiar to you, translating into larger talent pools, a larger customer base, and larger partner, vendor, and supplier networks.

As a basic rule, people are more drawn to an environment where they feel like others get them. And that sense of recognition builds enthusiasm that gets shared and multiplies. For example, imagine my surprise when the head of a university program I came through, which was led by an all-white faculty, approached me about becoming an instructor because, she acknowledged, representation among the faculty didn't come anywhere close to mirroring the diversity of the student body. This was a reality I was aware of from the moment I stepped in the classroom. But here was someone in a position of power who not only acknowledged it but was ready to start tackling the issue. That was a story I wanted to tell. It motivated me to start a dialogue among my personal alumni network of people who looked like me about putting ourselves forward to help solve a problem we long recognized. Starting that dialogue, in turn, gave the program access to a pool of people they wouldn't have reached otherwise.

That's just one example of cultural competence in action. Engaging people in a powerful way that honors their identity and experience can, in turn, build good will and compel your existing network to become your brand ambassadors in spaces where you're viewed as no different than any other organization. That same scenario could play out in the context of hiring, finding strategic partners for a venture, and discovering untapped markets and geographies, for example. And not only does cultural competence give your organization access, it also gives you credibility, which is critical to establishing meaningful connections to build from. The wins are exponential.

Broader Reach

> Operating with cultural competence amplifies your voice and signals to a broader audience that you're genuinely interested and invested in their voices and their needs.

While it has since become mired in controversy after controversy, the clothing brand Benetton serves as an example, in my memory, of a brand that designed campaigns that resonated with people of diverse backgrounds. In the early 90s, I didn't see any other brand so intentionally incorporating images of ethnically diverse people. And in my teenage fashion reality of the Gap and Express, the fact that I was aware of an Italian brand that was priced beyond my means says a lot. The brand's visuals resonated with people of color, and the awareness this created made it part of the lexicon. Even in recent years, I heard a contemporary of mine say their staff photo "looked like a Benetton ad," in that instance, a proud proclamation about the rich diversity among their team. (Note: That statement was made by a person of color.) This example illustrates the power of placing your brand, business, and product with cultural competence. When people see themselves in your story, it draws them to you and broadens your appeal. I've never heard any businessperson claim increased exposure was antithetical to their growth strategy.

Market Differentiation

> Cultural competence is a competitive
> advantage in an era when it's becoming
> common practice for people to take their
> talents and their dollars to organizations that
> value who they are.

At a time when employees are quitting their jobs in droves due to a misalignment of values, do you want to be the firm that people leave or the one they go to? At a point when younger generations, the workforce of tomorrow, are demanding change and questioning the norms of workplace culture, do you want to be the employer with a track record of flexibility and innovation or the one that's stuck in a past where people like them were unseen? At a point in history when diverse and respectful representation has become expected and online backlash is swift and severe, do you want to be the firm without people of color or people of different ages and abilities on your website? These are choices firms make, whether they recognize it or not, when they choose whether to adapt with respect for humanity and difference or stick with "the way we've always done things." And if you're not willing to adapt but your competitors are, these trends are a good indicator of where that will leave your firm.

Early Intervention

> A culturally competent group is likely to
> address potential issues before they're allowed
> to fester or spiral to levels that threaten
> psychological safety, team dynamics, individual
> reputation, and financial stability.

In a firm where the workforce understands and has an appreciation for difference, there is more likelihood and space for issues to be addressed when someone acts without respect for difference. Such an environment makes it easier to address it in the moment when a colleague uses an offensive term or cites a stereotype when designing apparel for a particular market segment, for example. Culturally competent people are more aware and equipped to appropriately address issues like these, which, if left unchecked, could be detrimental to individuals, your team, or ultimately your firm. Keep in mind, one poorly handled or overlooked microaggression could damage a team's sense of trust and safety in a way that could completely tank their productivity. And a single discrimination suit could cost your firm an average of $250K.

Internal Escalation

> A culturally competent organization is more likely to create space for issues to be escalated and addressed internally before they become public matters.

Just as interpersonal intervention is more likely to occur among a culturally competent workforce, ill-conceived products, images, or other issues are more likely to be escalated and addressed internally in a culturally competent firm. Let's say for example, a product team designs a device for older people that is challenging to use if you have dexterity issues. In a firm that takes time to understand the needs of the population they serve, someone on that team might catch the problem and address it with their manager. Or if the product makes it to the testing phase, maybe a quality control specialist would make the catch before it went into mass production. The point here is that a culture of appreciation and understanding of difference builds in multiple fail-safes that prevent an oversight in concept development from making it to distribution and into the hands of a customer and causing them real-life inconvenience or even harm. Creating a culture where people are empowered to speak up and advocate for the customer based on an understanding of their needs before a product goes to market can spare a firm from scandal, reputation damage, litigation, or far worse.

Alignment

> When cultural competence is centered in your firm and individuals are expected to live and be held accountable for living the values of DEIB, you create a consistent experience for your staff, as well as any external stakeholders they engage with.

Referring back to the DEIB Value Continuum, a firm cannot strive to build an external brand that claims to respect and value humanity while neglecting its staff. Similarly, it cannot focus all its DEIB efforts internally at the expense of the customers, partners, and communities they serve. Effectively operating with cultural competence means embodying an appreciation for difference and a respect for humanity that is experienced by every stakeholder your firm touches. That alignment conveys your integrity and signifies your commitment to operate with people's best interest at heart, which is what we all ultimately wish for.

Risks of Neglecting Cultural Competence

On the other side of the coin, there are significant risks to a firm that operates without cultural competence. Those risks include the following:

FIGURE 4—RISKS OF NEGLECTING
CULTURAL COMPETENCE

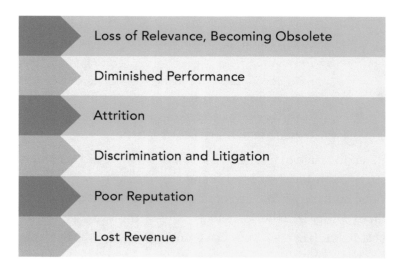

Loss of Relevance, Becoming Obsolete

Diminished Performance

Attrition

Discrimination and Litigation

Poor Reputation

Lost Revenue

Loss of Relevance, Becoming Obsolete

> A lack of cultural competence will prevent your firm from keeping pace with societal changes as your workforce, customers, and other stakeholders evolve.

You can look all around you and recognize how things are changing. Think about your own workforce, your neighborhood, your industry, and the schools you attended. The demographics of our society are changing, and they're becoming more diverse. Organizations that can adapt to our shifting culture and their shifting needs will thrive. The ones that appreciate this evolution are already ahead of the game. But the ones who lean in, get curious, and intentionally educate themselves and get comfortable with difference and change will maintain connections with existing stakeholders and position themselves to connect with new ones.

A prime example of a design field that must keep up with the pulse of society is fashion. Fashion is all about looking months and years into the future to predict and create trends. This fall's looks already went down the runway in the spring. Next spring's looks will be on runways this fall. The cycle from season to season is relentless. And if designers are not in tune with what people want and need, they can quickly fall out of favor. While other design fields may not operate on such a stringent calendar, none of them can afford to deny the passage of time. And designers cannot deny the fact that certain decisions are already being made for them based on culture shifts. The Color Marketing Group has been selecting our industries' palettes in response to our evolving world for decades. Pantone announces a color of the year every December inspired by current cultural and societal trends, and suddenly you see it everywhere. It's on us as designers to consciously adopt a similar approach — because no one wants to become the Kodak of culture.

Diminished Performance

> Low cultural competence leads to an overall lack of inclusion, which negatively impacts employees' drive and capacity to perform and contribute.

Stop and think about a time when you felt out of place. It may have been at the start of a new class or in your first client meeting or at your first industry event. Think about all the thoughts and feelings that coursed through your mind other than what you were there to do: anxiousness, hesitation, maybe even doubt. To take it a step further, imagine you and others who looked like you were clearly being treated differently. No one acknowledged you or asked your opinion, even if the topic of discussion pertained to people like you. Now imagine having that feeling every day *and* being expected to create something — and it better be good. Not only are you under duress, but you're expected to tap into the places in your heart, mind, and even your spirit to develop and deliver whatever your gift produces. No pressure, right?

Plenty of designers work under these conditions every day because their colleagues, their managers, and their leaders don't see, acknowledge, or value their identity. That should be very concerning to you. Imagine for a minute what these people could produce if all that occupied headspace was freed up. Imagine what they would contribute if they knew you, your team, and your organization cared about what they were experiencing and were willing to make adjustments to eliminate the barriers that stifle them. Going back to that memory of being in a new class, think about how your creative guards came down once you started connecting with a classmate or the instructor. Or once someone recognized your artistic ability.

Many design professionals are still waiting for that recognition and connection in their workplaces to this very day. Employees' performance is negatively impacted in places and spaces where they feel they do not belong. On the other hand, firms that honor people's identity by giving them a voice and acknowledging their talents tap into a whole new level of innovation, ideas, insights, and engagement. The firms that do not leave some very valuable knowledge and contributions on the table — at the expense of their business, their workforce, and their customers.

Attrition

> Employees will not stay where they do not feel seen or valued, especially if your competition is stepping up to the plate and operating in ways that honor their identity and perspectives.

How long do you think people want to stay in a space where they can't fully express themselves? As a creative, how much and how well can you create in an unwelcoming or uncomfortable environment? If you are treated unfairly, or if you feel you can't express or share relevant insight from your perspective and experience, or if you do and you're ignored, would you want to stay in that organization? This is what happens in firms with no cultural competence. Even if people find safe pockets — either a one-off team or leader who listens or even invites or celebrates them — that's not always enough to keep them there.

Good talent is hard, and costly, to find. So wouldn't you want to do your best to foster and nurture the talent you have? The key here is recognizing that your retention efforts aren't going to land the same with everyone. To maintain a staff of individuals, you have to meet a range of needs. You have a better chance of being successful if: 1) you recognize that everyone's needs are not the same, 2) you do the work to find out what's meaningful to people of different backgrounds, and 3) most importantly, you deliver that. We've heard it everywhere. Diversity of thought and experience breeds innovation. And businesses must innovate to survive. If you cannot retain diverse talent, you're missing out on opportunities to innovate. Meanwhile, the competitors that can attract and retain that talent will endure.

Discrimination and Litigation

> If your organization is uninformed about the nuances of cultural difference and operating with cultural competence, you open yourself up to creating a workplace culture that tolerates, turns a blind eye to, or fails to discourage discriminatory behavior.

This type of environment is fertile ground for claims of discrimination and, much worse, lawsuits. A common excuse that comes up when an offense or incident surfaces in an organization is "I didn't know." Someone "didn't know" a project manager had a habit of specifying lower quality finishes for affordable housing dwellings, saying "They're just going to destroy the place anyway." Someone "didn't know" that their firm paid design interns from predominantly white universities more than they paid interns from historically Black colleges and universities (HBCUs). Someone "didn't know" that employees who spoke with an accent were consistently overlooked for leadership positions that required presenting to clients.

In an environment that promotes cultural competence, these issues would be raised before they became patterns of behavior that could jeopardize a firm's very existence. These matters would be addressed because, more often than not, someone *does* know. They just don't feel they can safely raise the issue without jeopardizing their own career. Or even worse, they believe no one in a position of power will care, understand, or ultimately do anything about it. When there's no safe recourse, these things fester until they reach a point where someone is harmed, physically or psychologically, or the patterns become so egregious, they can no longer be swept under the rug. At that point, the only viable option often appears to be litigation.

Poor Reputation

> A lack of cultural competence can threaten your firm's reputation internally, among the workforce, and publicly, as an employer, a partner, and a corporate citizen.

This reputation damage could negatively impact the viability of your organization and potentially cost you employees, customers, sponsors, and more. Let's say you have a staff of one hundred people. Those one hundred people represent one hundred opportunities for you to develop spokespeople for your brand. And if, say, twenty percent of those people are people from underrepresented groups, they represent twenty opportunities for you to spread awareness of your brand among their networks, likely comprised of people who identify like those staff members do.

The environment, culture, and experience you foster can make your employees your ambassadors or your trolls. Word of mouth reaches far and wide — and at lightning speed thanks to the internet. And bad news seems to travel that much faster. So it's to your advantage to be known as the firm living up to the promises it made in the summer of 2020, for example, as opposed to the firm that claims diversity, equity, and inclusion as values but still has only one person of color on the executive leadership team. These things matter, and people, including your employees, your customers, and your competitors, are paying attention. Each of these groups plays a role in framing the story of your firm.

Lost Revenue

> A lack of cultural competence can limit your understanding of what's relevant to potentially viable customer bases and prevent you from ever accessing them.

You cannot tap into markets you don't bother to understand or even explore, let alone connect with. Traditional business thinking typically relies on data, analysis, and identified constraints to predict and fulfill customers' needs. As a proponent of design thinking, I believe in a different approach. I firmly believe in engaging directly with your customers to identify their challenges from their perspective and experience and then working with them to test ideas and solutions. This is human-centered design. It takes the guesswork out of expanding business lines and coming up with new products and service offerings because they're co-created *with* the customer in response to real, verified needs.

Increasingly, human-centered design is becoming the way to do business. Just ask Apple about their reliance on building and testing prototypes with end users. Or Nike, where employees and customers are invited into the design process to build innovative products and experiences. At the root of their approaches are human connection and human understanding. You only tap into these elements by understanding how people live, what's important to them, and what informs their perspectives and experiences. Hello, cultural competence.

Cultural competence can be your firm's competitive advantage if you use it to truly engage with different populations and get an understanding of their needs, so you can cater to them in ways they will find impactful, not ways you think they will find impactful. The latter comes with built-in blinders. Cultural competence equips your firm to upgrade from the golden rule of treating customers the way you would want to be treated to the platinum rule of treating them the way they want to be treated. Which do you think is going to set you up for long-term success? And which is your firm currently positioned to do?

Weighing the benefits of operating with cultural competence versus the risks of operating without it paints a clear picture. Choosing the latter is a costly proposition. There are ways to equip your workforce to minimize that risk. That's what we'll cover throughout the remaining chapters of this book. But before we get to how culturally competent designers show up, let's look at ways you can identify a culturally competent design firm.

Cultural Competence in Action

Certain practices come along with being a culturally competent design firm. In these firms, conversations about difference are not stifled. There is a freedom to respectfully ask questions about dimensions of humanity you're unfamiliar with. There is an expectation that you will raise concerns about conduct that could be considered offensive, and there's accountability for doing so. There is room and opportunity for discussion about cultural implications of design choices without fear of retribution. In short, these firms function with a culture of respect for the humanity of their peers and of the people they serve.

When it comes to identifying future talent, these firms make their best effort to mirror the diversity of their market. They want to make sure they bring voices into their design process that are representative of the populations they are designing for. They also understand the importance of creating opportunities for these individuals to engage with and co-create with clients and customers and to share diverse perspectives and encourage clients and customers to do the same.

In order to reach this talent, these firms also understand that they're not going to get different results using the same old sourcing and recruiting tactics. They recognize it may be worth asking their own staff about professional associations for people of color they belong to, or LGBTQ job boards they're familiar with, or veterans' forums they're plugged into. They understand the value of supporting, sponsoring, or partnering with strategically identified philanthropic organizations or educational institutions to organically build pipelines.

These firms don't limit their exploration of cultural differences to annual cultural observance programs held during a lunch break. They create opportunities for sharing stories and engaging in discussion, so their staff gets to learn about each other as individuals. They also broaden this scope by encouraging exploration and conversations about cultural factors to consider when designing for particular populations. They don't assume they have all the answers, so they collaborate with their clients and customers on these topics as well.

On a given day, there may be a respectful, constructive dialogue among colleagues about a design choice that could be perceived as culturally insensitive. There might be an instance when a team member is asked to weigh in on an aspect of a project based on an element of their identity because they've become accustomed to and comfortable freely discussing it.

There may be a healthy debate about a design concept and its interpretations ahead of a major client presentation.

These are all indicators of a firm operating with cultural competence. Some people may read these examples and think, *That doesn't sound so hard.* My question to them would be: If it's not that hard, why aren't you already doing it? Adopting cultural competence is not impossible, but it does require intention and transformational change. Others might say, "We already do some of that." However, pockets of cultural competence are not the same as an entire firm operating this way. Employees or clients shouldn't have a different experience based on the leader, team, or department in your firm they happen to encounter. Still others may say, "We're doing just fine operating the way we are," but few businesses survive by sticking to their norms and not adapting. As the saying goes, innovate or die. All the signs point to new ways of existing, from the pandemic to the Great Resignation to the heightened debate about social justice and the coexistence of four very distinct generations in the workforce. Culture is shifting, and the firms that can navigate that shift will win.

Scan this QR code to download a **discussion guide** for this chapter.

2

CULTURAL COMPETENCE FOR DESIGNERS

t is a gift to be able to design. As designers, we have the ability to translate concepts into beautiful and practical forms that only we could create. We draw from our talents and our experience and put our DNA into things that have never been seen before because they could only come from us.

Along with this gift comes great responsibility. Once we create something and it's out in the world, we have limited control over how it will be used or how it will be interpreted. Even when we design with one person in mind, like in the case of a commissioned artist, our creation will likely outlast the patron. Then who will it be good or useful or meaningful for?

By the same token, we cannot always control or account for what will become of our work. Despite our intentions or efforts, we run the very real risk that something we design could be controversial — and not in a buzzworthy, viral-sensation kind of way. Even worse, we could design something that could be harmful. In a very extreme example, heinous crimes were committed against women in an embattled area. Erectile dysfunction medication, originally manufactured to treat a medical condition, was used by the fighters to systematically rape and "conquer" women in the areas they invaded. I can't imagine the scientists in those labs ever envisioned a product they were developing would become a tool of such violence and horror. But this demonstrates the limited control over products we creators have once they are out of our hands.

I'm sure none of us wants to leave a legacy as the designer of a weaponized product. Or the designer of the memorial library dedicated to a historical figure with a previously undiscovered criminal past. Or the designer of a controversial logo that appalls and retraumatizes a whole demographic of a population.

Bottom line: Decisions we make as designers affect outcomes for people we factor into our designs, as well as those we don't. So what can we do about it? What is in our control is the ability to be as informed as we can before and while we are in the process of designing.

The Tools of Our Trade

Designers manipulate various elements to achieve a design, but if we are not careful of how we use them, we could create a product that does more of a disservice than a service. Certain tools in our designer toolkit are particularly relevant to the discussion of cultural competence. This is because nuances associated with them can vary according to one's background or beliefs. These tools include symbols and motifs, color, and imagery.

Symbols and Motifs

A friend recently shared with me a photograph from an interior designer's residential project for a Black client and asked me if anything stood out to me. At first glance, I was impressed by the rich color scheme, the luxe fabrics, the combination of classic and organic patterns, and the regal artwork, which included African sculptures. But then I saw it, a small decorative item among an assortment on the coffee table. It looked like links of a chain. I was suddenly fixated on this item and jarred by the disconnect between this space that oozed sophisticated reverence for culture and heritage and this one trinket that immediately brought to my mind literal bondage and enslavement.

As designers, we are very deliberate about the items we select and the compositions we create, so I wondered how that piece had made it into this space. I wondered if it was meant to make a statement of ironic triumphant juxtaposition or if it was something the client may have signed off on. But honestly, my first instinct was that the designer made a very tone-deaf design choice. I was actually disturbed to the point of wanting to track down the designer's contact information to ask for an explanation.

In that moment, another instance came to mind from a home renovation show I had recently watched. A designer was walking a Black couple through their newly completed, beautifully appointed home (which was devoid of much cultural flavor, very typical of most of the network shows, but I digress.) They got to the dining area, and what was hanging above the table? A sizable light fixture comprised mostly of thick, twisted rope. Once again, I had a very visceral reaction. I felt my face contort before the thought really formed in my head. But then the words came together: Why would you, a designer, choose to place hanging rope — rope hanging from the ceiling, no less — in the home of a Black family? In my mind, the association with lynching was automatic and concerning.

I call attention to these examples to drive home the importance of cultivating awareness and, yes, even sensitivity around the meaning behind symbols and motifs we incorporate into our work as designers. I cannot claim to know what reaction the clients had in either of these instances, but the fact that alarms went off for me as a Black woman goes to show these design choices were not without impact. I can't help wondering if the final selections could have been different if the dialogue in each of those design processes had been different. Were the designers unaware of how their choices could be interpreted? Did they make the same associations I made but allow their artistic preference to override their judgement? Did they think to get an opinion from a fellow designer or even the clients themselves? Was the dynamic they created with the client such that the client didn't feel comfortable voicing their opinion?

There's really no way of knowing, but these questions point to the duty of the designer to be curious, to be thoughtful, and to make decisions from an informed standpoint. Is it really appropriate to incorporate your interpretation of "tribal" patterns into every "ethnic" project? Do you even know what they mean? Are the patterns and visuals that come to mind when you think "Asian-inspired" anywhere close to accurately representing a monolith comprised of forty-eight individual countries? In this age of proliferating Pride Month product lines, are you aware that there is controversy about the use of the rainbow and its many variations among the LGTBQ community, the very one you claim to be honoring?

These examples involve associations based on race, ethnicity, and sexual orientation, but these are just a few dimensions of the identity of the clients we work with and for. The onus is on us to get to know them — beyond surface likes and dislikes — to really understand what resonates with them, their lifestyle, and their ways of being. It's up to us to use that information to help shape the solution we design for them. One step in that process may be explicitly inquiring about symbols and motifs you select or ones clients specifically want to avoid.

DESIGN GONE WRONG

Louis Vuitton Jamaican Heritage Sweater Controversy—February 2021

In February 2021, Louis Vuitton released a sweater to honor Jamaica.

The colors of the sweater are red, yellow, and green. But the colors of the Jamaican flag are actually yellow, green, and black.

An online uproar started with a tweet by user @pam_boy: (@pam_boy) "I cannot stress enough how important it is to implement diversity as a value and not a symbol within fashion companies." (*Twitter*, February 2, 2021. https://bit.ly/3V1IBr6)

As if the original offense of misrepresentation was not damaging enough, it was followed by additional misinformed statements and actions. When the sweater went on sale, it was named a "Jamaican striped sweatshirt," and the description read "Jumper with a striped design inspired by the national flag of the Caribbean island." So what was the solution? The word "flag" was changed to "cultural heritage." Still not accurate.

Things heated up on social media again with tweets like this from user @DanniMaig: (@DanniMaig) "So @LouisVuitton attempted to fix it without properly researching AGAIN. These colors do not represent the heritage of the island as much of the heritage of Rastafarianism and the Rastafari movement that took place in Jamaica in the 1930s."

Source: *Twitter*, February 2, 2021.
❧ https://bit.ly/3VoYrvL

Louis Vuitton ultimately pulled the sweater from the website and later issued a statement, but public sentiment was clearly behind the need for increased diversity, cultural competence, and, therefore, awareness in the design process.

(Note: The Louis Vuitton website features a statement on fostering diversity and inclusion, as well as related ongoing actions that include, "Training 100% of our employees in the prevention of unconscious bias and stereotypes by 2022.")

Sources

❧ https://www.blackenterprise.com/louis-vuitton-completely-fumbles-its-homage-to-jamaica-in-latest-menswear-collection/

❧ https://hellobeautiful.com/3284411/louis-vuitton-jamaican-sweater-wrong-colors/

❧ https://us.louisvuitton.com/eng-us/magazine/articles/fostering-diversity-and-inclusion-2020#

Color

As a design student, I could not wait to get to the class about color. I had an obsession going back to my first box of sixty-four crayons. (So many options! So many combinations!) But then the lessons on color theory came and went — and that was it. I wanted to dive into color psychology and the physiological effects of color. And I knew there was more I didn't even know I should learn. When were we going to talk about the complexities of color, which can make or break our designs?

Fast forward to my color education through Frank Mahnke, one of my color mentors, and the IACCNA, which I pursued in parallel with my graduate program in interior design, and, several years into my design career, the eye-opening experience led by world-renowned color expert Leatrice Eiseman at the Eiseman Center for Color Information & Training. I got to learn all I'd anticipated learning about color and more. And the topic I'm most often drawn back to in the context of designing with cultural competence is cultural association with color.

Out of all the elements at our disposal, color may prompt the strongest responses. Show clients a mockup of a print ad, a mood board, or a demo of a new app, and I can guarantee some of them won't get past the color scheme. The thing designers should be aware of — and get ahead of, if at all possible — is that these responses can go way deeper than personal preference. Cultural associations with color are critical for designers in the bridal industry, for example. A traditional wedding gown color in America is white because of its association with purity. In China, however, where white attire happens to be associated with mourning, wedding gowns are traditionally red, which represents happiness and good fortune. And in Italy, the color purple is avoided in the context of anything bridal because in that culture purple is associated with funerals.

You may have been aware of these facts, but what's significant to note are the deeper meanings of color in different cultural contexts. Take skin color, for example. Across the globe, lighter skin tones have been held as the standard of beauty. Even the generic "nude" has, by default, been a white skin tone. Only recently has this trend started to evolve in response to heightened demand and the business world's awakening to the realities of the existing consumer population as referenced in Chapter 1. Now we see variations of "nude" in everything from multi-skin tone Band-Aids and emojis to ballet slippers and high heels.

This change is way overdue. It's just now becoming a topic of discussion among design teams to intentionally incorporate people of different skin tones into their renderings. I'm also finding it increasingly simple to locate multiethnic stock images to use for social media templates and business presentations. (Note: I take these as signs of progress but mere beginnings. We have a long way to go.)

But baby, we have come a long way when it comes to gender and color. It finally seems to be sinking in that pink and pastels are not, in fact, the only options available to represent the female gender. Bic learned this the hard way when they released their slim pink and lavender Bic for Her pens back in 2011. The product reviews alone are worth the search. While several expressed snarky relief at having pens suited for their small hands, many joked about the helpfulness of having products color-coded, so they know which ones are appropriate for women. The shifting and expanding conversations about gender are signs that designers have to expand our palettes. From the $511 billion beauty industry and the $2 trillion fashion industry to the more than $10 billion baby products market and everything in between, there are serious design decisions to be made and potentially significant implications to limiting our treatment and use of color to convey gender.

The responsible use of color is also critical in terms of accessibility. Color can be a powerful tool for conveying information, but to design equitably for people whose color perception is impacted by colorblindness (reduced ability to distinguish between colors) or age (the cornea yellows with age and impacts our color perception), for example, we have to be mindful of how we use it. As I found out while doing web design for a federal agency, there are regulations in place to ensure websites and other information and communications technology are accessible to people with disabilities. Some of these regulations specifically address color. Section 508 of the Rehabilitation Act specifies that color cannot be the sole means of conveying information (e.g., web links are a different color *and* underlined) and that sufficient color contrast is required. It's not just the selection of colors that makes a designer culturally competent. It's also knowledge of their nuances.

Color can be used to make people and their identities feel seen. Conversely, when misused, it can offend or even ostracize and exclude. It is our duty as designers to explore color and its many dimensions to ensure we're using it responsibly.

DESIGN GONE WRONG

**Spanish Postal Service
"Equality Stamps"—May 2021**

In May of 2021, the Spanish postal service, Correos España, issued a set of four stamps in different skin-colored tones called "Equality Stamps." According to NPR, the postal service introduced them on the anniversary of George Floyd being killed by a police officer in Minneapolis. The purpose was to make a statement against racial inequality. The intent was that the stamps "reflect an unfair and painful reality that shouldn't be allowed" and that every letter or parcel sent with them would "send a message against racial inequality." The campaign was launched during European Diversity Month in collaboration with Spain's national SOS Racism Federation, a nonprofit group.

The issue with the stamps wasn't directly tied to the colors chosen but to the fact that the darker the tone, the lower the monetary value of the stamp. This sent a message that there was greater value attributed to people with lighter skin tones.

Backlash ensued.

To make matters worse, the controversy was addressed with a divided voice. In an egregious lack of accountability, Correos España said it would make no comment on the controversy. Meanwhile, NPR reported the Madrid contingent of supporting organization SOS Racismo said, "The campaign helps conceal the structural nature of racism and perpetuate the notion of Black inferiority."

The campaign received severe criticism on social media. Sales started on May 25 and shut down on May 28.

One of the many issues to focus on in this example is that at some point in the development of this campaign, someone made the decision to assign values in this way, and ultimately a designer placed those values on the stamp images themselves. According to SOS Racismo Madrid, "Any racially aware person would have identified what was wrong with the campaign... The blunder proved the need for more racially aware people in decision-making positions at companies."

Source:

% https://www.npr.org/2021/05/28/1001228126/spains-new-postage-stamps-were-meant-to-call-out-racism-instead-they-drew-outrag

Imagery

Body type. Attire. Settings. Environment. All of these variables play into the overall impact of a design. Stop and think for a moment: Whose images are you incorporating into your work and in what context?

Sitting in a Joe's Crab Shack several years back, I examined the space, as interior designers are prone to do. The eatery was filled with typical chain restaurant décor — knickknacks displayed on the walls, old photographs used throughout the space. Then I looked closely at the images incorporated into the tabletop design. There I saw a postcard depicting a public lynching in the good old U.S. of A. Right there on full unapologetic display. I was infuriated, wondering how that ever could have made it to a chain restaurant establishment. But now as I write these words, I have to ask not only who in the production process didn't yank that image, but also who *designed* that collage in the first place and thought that the image of a lynching was suitable to use. (Side note: The news story you will find in relation to this controversy calls out a Roseville, Minnesota, location. In 2016, the Minneapolis NAACP chapter demanded a corporate apology from the chain, and the image was removed. I encountered the image in a Washington, DC, metro location around the same time period, indicating the exponential reach of such offenses when they're made within large organizations.)

Source

🔗 https://www.usatoday.com/story/news/nation-now/
2016/03/11/joes-crab-shack-lynching-photo-texas-
hanging-table-decor/81633822/

Speaking of large organizations, it finally clicked for PepsiCo in 2020 that the image of Aunt Jemima was not okay. The brand's image started in the late 1800s with a mammy who didn't lose her head scarf until 1989. But please don't be misled into thinking that was a suitable compromise or that the controversy around what the logo represented didn't start until a century into its existence. It just took that much time for any change to be made. Ultimately, it took the on-camera murder of George Floyd in 2020 to completely revamp the brand. In the midst of the corporate social awakening that followed, PepsiCo felt motivated to change the image and the name. So now we have the Pearl Milling Company.

But is that what it takes for design to honor humanity? A worldwide outcry for justice? I would argue that the answer is no. If designers own their agency in the creation and curation of images in the first place, we can play a critical part in shifting the narrative and aligning our craft with the turning tides of our culture. And as in the cases of symbols and color, we have to expand our awareness of the multiple facets that make up our identities to responsibly use imagery. We have to ask ourselves if the artwork we specify for a community health facility resonates with the actual people living in that community. Or if the images we incorporate into a fashion app properly reflect what real people's bodies look like. (Fashion is slowly making advances in this regard, but it's still an indication of where things stand when the contestants on shows like *Project Runway* cringe when they get the plus-sized models. Last time I checked, people of all sizes still need clothes to wear.)

This is what it means when you hear "representation matters." The images we choose send very real messages about who's welcomed in and who's shut out, about who's respected and valued and who's not. It's on us to choose carefully.

The Designer's Hero Complex

Designers possess very special gifts. With our own unique inspiration, we translate concepts into forms the world can see, feel, and experience. We perceive things differently. We interpret things differently. We bring creations and solutions into the world that spill over with creativity.

To do this, we often feel we must be given a certain degree of latitude to articulate our own visions and to fold our own interpretations into the final product. While I appreciate that, there are some parameters to our process that we must respect. Those parameters come into play when our work explicitly requires incorporating signifiers of our customer's identity.

Let's think through a couple scenarios that illustrate this point. Say you have a client who shares that their vision is to appeal to an urban market and that's the feel they want you to achieve in what you create for them. If you're in fashion, the first thing that comes to mind for you may be the fly looks you see on kids at trendy spots around town. If interiors are your thing, you might check out the scene in a hot, up-and-coming neighborhood in New York City. You might follow the socials for a cutting-edge metropolitan digital publication if you're looking for some graphic design inspiration.

These are all logical starting points, and by no means is this handful of examples meant to be an exhaustive list. But it's the next step in the process — what we as designers do with this inspiration — that requires examination. Do we take that and translate it into our personal interpretation of "urban" for our client? Do we forge down a path of designing options that resonate with our individual understanding? Do we possibly even incorporate our own nod to "urban" in the final product as a surprise for the client because we find it to be so clever?

Or do we take a step back and intentionally carve out time to co-create this urban concept with the client before we dive into solutions?

It can be very easy to get caught up in buzzwords, our own creative process, and our individual frame of reference when we are designing. But we can't leave our clients and their customers' perspectives out of the equation. It's not just about what you want me to design, but also who you want me to design it for. In this instance, that sounds like asking what the client's interpretation of urban is. Is it tied to geography? Urban areas in the midwest United States are a lot different than urban areas in the southeast, for example. Not to mention the variety among urban areas across the globe. Is urban tied to someone's stereotypical notion of what urban areas are like (i.e., Black)? Are they talking about socioeconomically disadvantaged, drug-and-violence-infested, scrappy urban? Or newly gentrified, walkable, Millennial urban?

The true test is determining how much your concepts resonate with the customers. Do they see themselves in what you're creating? Do they somehow feel celebrated in the solution you're framing? At the very least, do they feel it's an accurate representation? These are the answers that matter, not how elaborate you got in your design or how artistically you think you represented an idea. It's ultimately about how effectively you translate cultural concepts in ways that uplift versus tear down. The only way to really get there is to go straight to the source and seek out those insights in your design process.

BOOST YOUR
CULTURE QUOTIENT

Perspectives from a Design Educator

Name: Bill Allen

Occupation: Professor of Fashion Design & Production Management

Q: How do you describe your role in design?

A: I prepare fashion designers to be technically sound as they enter the very competitive fashion industry. My role as a fashion designer is to design simple but well-constructed garments for the masses of people. I like to design garments that can go from daywear to night to evening wear by adding the proper accessories, etc.

Q: How has your industry experience influenced what you teach fashion students?

A: As a former director of business development for the AbilityOne program, I helped to acquire $400 million in contracts with contractors that employed people with disabilities and manufactured high-quality military attire for the Warfighter. At least fifteen percent of the world's population have some type of disability, so this is an important market to consider. This point is communicated and emphasized to our students. One in four U.S. adults (61 million people) live with a disability, according to cdc.gov.

Q: You shared that your own experience as a design student had a big impact on your career. What contributed to the inclusive environment you experienced as a student?

A: While a student at FIT, I met people from all around the world of different races, religions, and creeds, along with various sexual preferences. I am still friends with many of them today.

Some designers feel our artistic license entitles us to create from our own sources of inspiration and motivation, unencumbered by any type of restrictions or rules. While I get this sentiment, it does not have to be diametrically opposed to or exclusive of engaging with the people we design for to find out what's truly meaningful to them. Culturally competent designers recognize the importance of balancing our expression as designers with the expression of our customers' identity. We owe them that.

Some designers may ask, "But isn't that someone else's job? Why can't we just create and then hand it off to someone in charge of marketing or quality control or someone more senior to review our work?" That's like a reporter throwing together a sloppy story because they assume a fact checker is going to go behind them and verify the details. That does not absolve the reporter of accountability to do their own due diligence. You are the designer. You are ground zero. There would be nothing to check if you never created it. Yes, there are many players involved in the creative process for a reason, but the greatest responsibility lies with the creator.

Deficiencies in Design Education

Most of us get our formal introduction to design through the hallowed halls of academia. Design school is the great equalizer, the place where we get our foundational education about our design specialty before entering our respective professions. But that foundation is problematic because, by and large, design education does not incorporate the identities, experiences, and work of anyone other than those of the dominant culture.

Why is this problematic? For one thing, our educational experience forms the basis for our understanding of our profession. It's where we learn the basic concepts and tools of our trade. It's where we're supposed to learn what makes a "good" designer. It's our boot camp, where our expectations of the norms, protocols, and rules of engagement are established — both in the classroom and through experiences like internships. Our educational experience signals to us a lot about what is important in design. And if you look at what we're taught, it seems design is only important for white people, people of moderate to high socioeconomic status, and maybe a sampling of "special populations" that don't even comprise the breadth of ability. Accordingly, when the voices of historically excluded people are not folded into the curriculum or even acknowledged in the room, that speaks volumes.

So yes, I am calling out design education as the primary point of failure in developing culturally competent designers. And here's why:

- lack of diversity in the curriculum
- lack of diversity among faculty
- lack of identity acknowledgment in the classroom
- lack of identity acknowledgement in the design process

If my learning was restricted to what I learned in my design program, I would have thought interior design revolved around white people. All the signals I got told me it was a profession for white people and that designers design for white people. My educational experience would also have led me to believe the only dimensions of humanity a designer needed to be prepared to factor into their work were ability and maybe age. Even these were addressed in the context of specialized spaces, as if people of varying abilities and age do not occupy the same spaces as the majority. The one human-centered design specialty we formally learned about was universal design and that specifically focuses on accessibility. (Reminder: The dimensions of humanity also include race, ethnicity, gender, sexual orientation, age, class, and religion, among others.) I could have easily walked away from my program with this limited perspective based on the lack of diversity in the curriculum, at the front of the classroom, and in our dialogue. It was as if there was a sign posted that said for all "others" to leave their identity at the door.

Let's take a look at what a disservice this type of education does for students. Overall, it cheats them out of a critical opportunity to broaden their frame of reference. As designers, we don't generally get to choose who we design for. And even if we did, we could never presume to understand everything about our customers' identities that would be important to fold into our design. So when our initial exposure to design fails to require us to even examine the importance of identity, this automatically puts us at a disadvantage.

And how do we overlook identity? For one, we don't study designers of different backgrounds. People from a particular cultural background who have lived experience in that culture are the best people to learn from. They can convey both spoken and unspoken beliefs, practices, and norms that you simply can't get from reading or even from observing in limited encounters. So why not study their work, their stories, their paths, and their approaches? It doesn't take much time, effort, or searching to find diverse designers to incorporate into existing courses. It doesn't take much effort to ask students of different backgrounds to share the names and work of designers they may be familiar with. That kind of information could be crowd-sourced in one class.

We also overlook identity when we fail to hire diverse faculty to teach in design programs. People of different backgrounds inherently bring different perspectives and experiences to a topic. They also bring an authenticity that cannot be achieved by others relaying accounts of their stories. I've often heard about the challenges finding people of color to teach in design programs, and I've even been approached about teaching myself.

I counter those claims that it's too hard to find diverse faculty with these questions:

1. Where are you searching? There are entire professional networks of Black designers, for example. Is anyone reaching out directly to these groups? Are you informing your existing student body about education as a career path? Your future faculty may be right in front of you.

2. Why should they teach at your institution? Are there other efforts happening to indicate that you have a vested interest in and commitment to not only bringing in diverse faculty but also setting them up to succeed and advance professionally there?

3. What type of environment are you welcoming them into? Are you inviting them into a space where other people who look like them are thriving? Will they be given the latitude to truly integrate their voice and experience into the curriculum in ways they find meaningful? Will they be teaching core courses or relegated to electives? And will their positions be in peril if a new department chair comes in?

BOOST YOUR
CULTURE QUOTIENT

Perspectives from a Design Educator

Name: Donna Kacmar

Occupation: Architect + Educator + Writer

Q: How do you describe your role in design?

A: In design I try to approach problems by finding the most minimal solution — in terms of size, cost, and impact. This is also how I approach teaching.

Q: What practices do you use to teach students how to design with customers' cultural identity in mind?

A: I am embracing learning with students and creating a safe place for discussion about what we are reading and watching, including:

- *Design Justice: Community-Led Practices to Build the Worlds We Need* by Sasha Costanza-Chock

- *Invisible Women: Data Bias in a World Designed for Men* by Caroline Criado Perez

- *Red Alert!: Saving the Planet with Indigenous Knowledge* by Daniel Wildcat

- *Design for the Other 90%* by Barbara Bloemink and Cynthia E. Smith

- Chimamanda Ngozi Adichie's TedX talk, "The Danger of a Single Story"

- *Urbanized*, documentary by Gary Hustwit

In design studio, I am adding a broader range of readings, plus talking with students about how to understand a site and context more fully. I encourage them to attend community events as a way to learn about the culture of the area. I am planning on organizing more service-related events throughout the academic year to learn by engaging with urban spaces. For instance, we are teaming with a group to do a sidewalk audit that can help support a more diverse and equitable transportation system in car-oriented cities, such as Houston.

Q: What's one thing design programs could start doing right now to ensure students factor cultural identities into their work?

A: The first thing we can do in design programs is sit and listen to both our students and our communities. Getting to know each other is the first step. That takes patience and generosity of spirit. Then we can work on building trust through effective communication strategies that enable us to make decisions together.

This communication must be open and transparent. Holding on to outdated power systems does not help. Communication also requires that we have a shared vocabulary and understand terminology together.

The state of the environment also dictates the extent to which the identities of the students are addressed in design courses. When instructors are oblivious, ignorant, or hesitant to address the identities of the students in the room, they deny those students the chance to express themselves and their reality in their work. In turn, they deny the entire class — and themselves — potential learning opportunities. In another vein, instructors who profess to be open to such input and then either question or dismiss the knowledge those students share do another kind of damage. Their unwillingness to accept others' realities wounds those individuals who courageously chose to share in the first place, breeding mistrust and limiting self-expression.

To take it a step further, students of any background or group who are never taught to account for identity in the design process are also left at a disadvantage. This deficit is at the core of what we'll explore in the rest of this book, but its roots are in the design process we learn as students. At some point, we have to learn the importance of understanding and appreciating difference among the people we design for. At some point, we have to learn where in the design process we should start asking in-depth questions about who will occupy the space, wear the garment, read the package, or use the app we're designing. At some point, we have to learn how we can contribute to an environment where these topics can be raised bravely and discussed openly and where solutions are informed by real-life experience and not by assumptions.

Scan this QR code to download a **discussion guide** for this chapter.

BOOST YOUR
CULTURE QUOTIENT

Perspectives from a Design Educator

Name: Jessica Bonness

Occupation: Assistant Professor, Interior Design

Q: How do you describe your role in design?

A: I am a certified interior designer and full-time educator, and previously I owned a residential practice for over ten years.

I teach primarily in the areas of ID foundation skills, design thinking, human-centered design (which is interdisciplinary, within the School of Design and Art), and career readiness and professional practice (including internships). My scholarship and research is tied to the teaching and learning that occurs in my classroom, and at the moment, I am interested in enhancing equity and belonging in academic and early career settings. I facilitate robust involvement of practitioners and industry professionals in the academic environment, with the goals of strengthening soft skills and creating relationships between students and industry, creating meaningful and equitable interactions, and educating and modeling best practices.

Q: What practices do you use to teach students how to design with customers' cultural identity in mind?

A: Immersive, inclusive research is essential for students to conduct when they begin a project. The immersion needs to be meaningful, and that can be intimidating or feel impossible to educators who admittedly aren't experts on everything, but it really shouldn't be. There are so many good resources out there today that educators can consult to bring diverse perspectives and rich cultural understanding into their classrooms, and if an educator is unfamiliar with them, they should make it a goal to ask for help in building their cultural resource library. For example, TED Talks, articles, and even blogs or Twitter feeds provide topical and current views. These types of media are equitable, too, because they are free and accessible. This approach does, however, put a serious responsibility on the educator to stay current and engaged and connected to the pulse of meaningful DEIB issues. If you do this right, you're modeling it for your students, and they will repeat it when they shift into practice. That's not overnight change with regard to industry, but it's going to create change in time.

Q: What methods have you used to invite students to incorporate their lived experience into their designs?

A: In 2021, my colleague Sal Pirrone and I had a great experience in a Foundation Studio where we broadened the topic selection approach to our final project, a memorial, to allow students to choose anything they wished to explore. Anything! What happened was instead of students designing memorials to commemorate the Triangle Shirtwaist Factory Fire (a notable event, but how many contemporary students truly connect with that?) they chose topics such as [the murder of] George Floyd, bipolar disorder, and Black women's hair. It was eye-opening how diverse the students' choices were, both in terms of topic but also in terms of the degree of vulnerability they were willing to embrace (which we need to make room for because not everyone wants to share their deepest pain or most closely held values with their classmates).

3

SIX HABITS OF CULTURALLY COMPETENT DESIGNERS

Designing with cultural competence does not happen in a bubble. To really work, it requires an environment and systems steeped in cultural awareness and respect for humanity. It requires a collective mindset and behavior shift among individuals who commit to approach their craft differently and team up to bring about different outcomes for historically excluded people. The six habits of culturally competent designers are necessary to make that shift happen.

Design firms are comprised of individuals. The systems that have normalized design without cultural competence are ultimately upheld and enforced by individuals. So it stands to reason that some level of reflection and change is required on the part of individual designers to embrace designing with cultural competence. The next critical step for designers who resonate with the concepts described in Chapter 2 is to adopt the six habits described in this chapter, so they can lead by example and build the momentum necessary to get their colleagues on board.

Scan this QR code to download the **Six Habits of Culturally Competent Designers**.

FIGURE 5—SIX HABITS OF
CULTURALLY COMPETENT DESIGNERS

Habit #1	Take accountability
Habit #2	Ask questions
Habit #3	Seek knowledge
Habit #4	Talk to customers
Habit #5	Believe people
Habit #6	Share experience

Habit #1 Take Accountability

Culturally competent designers call attention to culturally insensitive missteps. They don't wait for someone else to catch the issue or assume someone else will speak up. When I first started talking about cultural competence with designers, I was surprised at how often they had been in situations where they could see the train wreck coming. They were part of a team that designed something racially insensitive or just flat out inaccurate, for example, and they never spoke up.

Many factors can contribute to this resistance or hesitation on the part of the individual designer. As a person of color, I identify with a fear of retribution, retaliation, insult, complete and utter dismissal, or being labeled as "sensitive" or some sort of troublemaker in these situations. In many spaces where we work, people of color are vastly in the minority, possibly even the only one who looks like us on a team or in an organization. And that can be a lonely, awkward, and scary place to exist. So there are a lot of factors to consider before calling attention to a design misstep, even if we are one hundred percent sure disaster lies ahead.

In these instances, other people on that team may also have a clue, even if they're members of the majority. But they may also have similar fears about the reaction they'll get if they speak up. Or it may simply be the case that a team member feels like they're too new to the team to say something or it's "not their place" to speak up because they're unsure if what they're perceiving is truly out of line. Maybe no one has ever raised these issues among the team, so not even seasoned team members are willing to step out and do things differently.

These are all valid concerns, but as long as we keep leaning on them, we will never make progress in producing more culturally competent designs. The people who will change the game will be the ones who bravely speak up and bring attention to the elephant in the room before it gets out. Yes, there is a certain comfort in silence and even in assuming someone else will do it, imagining that somewhere down the line, somebody will raise their hand and object before a client lays eyes on the product or, even worse, it's circulated freely among the public. But can we really take comfort when we allow any level of harm that could have been avoided if we had put our foot down in the first place? A culturally competent designer takes ownership and asks the tough questions as soon as they arise.

Habit #2 — Ask Questions

Culturally competent designers raise questions to make space for the exploration of cultural implications of design decisions. Sometimes we don't know what we don't know, which makes it important to rely on the knowledge of the other individuals in the room. We can never really know what insights or experiences other people may have until we ask questions. A simple one to incorporate into most any design process is: Have we considered all perspectives? It's broad, it's unassuming, and it welcomes input. The act of asking the question can be very powerful. The act of revisiting the original design and making changes based on the responses to that question is even more powerful.

In the course of making space for this dialogue, two major things happen. One, humility and vulnerability are conveyed in acknowledging that others may have input that has not been voiced. This communicates respect and a desire to hear from others besides the loudest people in the room. Two, acting upon the newly surfaced knowledge indicates that the additional perspectives are actually valued. This sets the stage for engagement on new and deeper levels, ultimately benefiting both the team and the customer.

Habit #3 — Seek Knowledge

Culturally competent designers do their research to find out about cultures and backgrounds that are different from their own. They invest the time to look beyond the information that's been fed to them or what they've generally accepted to be true. They seek out the voices of people with lived experience. They read their books, listen to their podcasts, attend their webinars, and watch their documentaries. They challenge the theories and stereotypes they learned in school. They engage with colleagues of different backgrounds in their own organizations. They lean into their curiosity and open their minds to receive different stories.

They actively pull the information they gather into their work as a designer. They use it to help frame questions for their clients and customers. They look into how other designers have learned to revere different identities in their work and how cultures and customs can be interpreted in forms, spaces, and objects. They do this because they understand that design informed by assumptions, instead of facts, instantly reads as inauthentic and that inauthenticity can cost them clients and credibility in the blink of an eye.

Culturally competent designers view knowledge seeking as a lifelong exercise. They understand society and culture are not static, and they do their best to keep up with the ways these shifts will impact their work. Take demographics, for example. The U.S. Census projects that our nation will be majority minority by the 2040s. Considering that the majority generally establishes the norms, that's just one indicator of big shifts on the way. And then there are the new schools of thought and ways of being each new generation brings. As humans, we are all in a constant state of transition, so as professionals who design for humans, designers have to keep pace. Culturally competent designers are in touch with this reality and fully embrace it.

They also recognize that while it is impossible to know absolutely everything about everyone, a little cultural competence goes a long way when it comes to expanding their customer base and venturing into new markets. Past projects or even branding that reads as out of touch or myopic could take some designers out of the running for new work before they even try to set up a meeting. Showing up with some level of cultural awareness can be a game changer, professionally, especially as the makeup of leadership and decision makers continues to evolve.

Habit #4 — Talk to Customers

Culturally competent designers don't presume to know what is culturally meaningful to their customers. They engage with them directly when possible, and they do their homework ahead of time to frame the conversation to be sure they will walk away with information that results in a culturally relevant and accurate end product. This is not to say designers have to be ethnographers trained to be cultural specialists and observers or even to say that designers have to be experts at facilitating dialogue. But those who can perform similar functions with some level of skill will be more likely to surface insights that result in a design that resonates with end users.

So what might that look like? Let's take a culturally competent interior designer, for example. They would evaluate a client's existing space to see how the customer's identity is represented in that space, taking note of things like imagery, symbols, and spaces dedicated to specialized functions. They would note how hierarchy of certain elements of identity are established, like spacious private offices for executives beside small, cramped cubes in a corporate space, or displays featuring young models in a store for a retailer that claims to be multigenerational. They would ask customers questions like: "How do you see yourself reflected in the existing space?" and "What about your identity or background do you want to see celebrated in the new space?"

Bottom line: Culturally competent designers do more than study data and demographics that clients or market researchers provide to them. They perform their own thoughtful analysis and go directly to the source to get information that will help them shape custom solutions. They lean into their humanity and keep in mind that they're designing for real people, not just customer profiles. And they interact with them accordingly.

Habit #5 **Believe People**

When culturally competent designers ask people to share their insights and experiences, they believe them. There is nothing more disingenuous than to seek insights and perspectives from someone based on their own lived experience, and then move forward with your interpretation of their truth. In addition to being insulting, disrespectful, and dismissive, this behavior also conveys that the person doing the asking ultimately views themself as the authority despite not having the experience of the person they asked. Culturally competent designers do all they can to avoid acting in this way.

This habit is critical to remember when it comes to gathering information from anyone, whether it's a customer, a colleague, or an acquaintance. It means that, as a designer, you take personal insights for what they are. If you have more questions, you ask instead of drawing your own conclusions. If you're not sure you effectively translated a concept into your design, you get input before you go further. If information you receive is outside your frame of reference and seems odd or makes you uncomfortable, you don't simply disregard it. If anything, those instances tell you to take note of what you find so personally challenging, so you can do your own work and explore that for yourself. Culturally competent designers seek to learn and grow from the new knowledge they acquire, and they accept other people's truth for what it is.

Habit #6 ▸ **Share Experience**

Culturally competent designers contribute their relevant personal or professional experience to the design dialogue. Just like Habit #1, I recognize that this habit requires a level of vulnerability on the part of individuals who tend to be excluded in the first place. But there is also nothing more powerful than firsthand accounts and insights when it comes to designing with cultural competence. I can't presume to know the temperature of anyone's professional environment — whether it's hostile or inviting, flexible or inflexible, old school or progressive. What I do know is that the most innovative environments are those in which people are encouraged to show up as their true, authentic selves, and those organizations are made up of individuals bold enough to heed the call. They know the dialogue will not change unless they add their voices to it. They acknowledge there may be a risk in being transparent, but they believe the outcome for customers, their colleagues, and future generations is worth it.

Culturally competent designers who show up in this way don't necessarily have to be lived experiencers themselves. They could also be those individuals who share insights they heard from others, possibly in similar contexts on other projects. By chiming in and helping to normalize these types of conversations, these designers can be just as instrumental in creating a safe environment for sharing personal experience.

These are just some of the fundamental habits of designers with cultural competence. As previously mentioned, when they are adopted on an individual basis, they can start setting the tone for more culturally competent design on a broader scale. I invite anyone who can envision themselves showing up in these ways to go a little deeper in the next chapter to truly process what it looks like when a collective of like-minded designers commits to cementing these habits into practice.

Scan this QR code to download a **discussion guide** for this chapter.

4

THE
CULTURAL
COMPETENCE
SHIFT

Transforming a design organization into one that prioritizes cultural competence requires a big shift. It's not enough for a firm to proclaim they will operate with cultural competence, and it's definitely not enough for just a handful of designers to take this on individually. For there to be significant transformation at a meaningful scale, culturally competent practices will have to be adopted and executed by entire teams throughout organizations. This is the only way to achieve consistency, integrity, and impact for people who have been historically excluded.

This kind of real change sends strong signals — both externally and internally. For one, it communicates a clear stance to your customers and stakeholders. Having a selection of stories to tell across a range of projects about the outcomes of your culturally competent approach is way more effective and memorable than any social justice statement or tweak to your mission statement. And this combination of consistency, integrity, and impact also demonstrates both commitment and expectations to your staff. Those same stories set a standard for what your collective organization stands for and what distinguishes your brand of design. It also communicates that the firm values identity and experience, which encourages genuine expression and collaboration and, ultimately, yields innovation.

For teams to make this shift to cultural competence, they have to transform in three fundamental areas:

1. Mindset

2. Environment

3. Behavior

The Mindset Shift

Nothing else can change without a shift in mindset. Any efforts made without an understanding of the significance of this shift will fall flat and will be performative at best because action without knowledge is empty. It will be perceived as disingenuous by the people you are attempting to acknowledge and include. And how will they be able to tell a change is genuine if there's been no clear articulation of why the change is happening? If a handful of leaders appear to be on board but their own managers don't say or do anything different to demonstrate a change in their outlook, you have a problem. If the firm's commitment waivers when anyone challenges a decision or an action they take, that response is inconsistent with a culturally competent mindset.

There are specific mindset shifts we have to make as designers in order to fully show up in the ways that the cultural competence shift requires as shown in Figure 6. The first is a willingness to be vulnerable. One of the most powerful acknowledgements an individual can make is "I don't know." Accepting that there are backgrounds and lifestyles you know nothing about is the most basic step in reversing the mindset that makes this book necessary. It signifies that you acknowledge you are not the authority on others' lives and lifestyles. It shows you respect those people enough to not make assumptions on their behalf, or even worse, to erase their identity by imposing your own simply out of ignorance and laziness. Following that up with action and inquiry signals a sincere desire to learn more about people you don't understand.

FIGURE 6—CULTURALLY COMPETENT MINDSET SHIFT

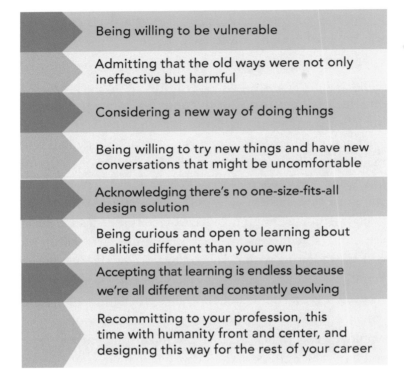

Being willing to be vulnerable

Admitting that the old ways were not only ineffective but harmful

Considering a new way of doing things

Being willing to try new things and have new conversations that might be uncomfortable

Acknowledging there's no one-size-fits-all design solution

Being curious and open to learning about realities different than your own

Accepting that learning is endless because we're all different and constantly evolving

Recommitting to your profession, this time with humanity front and center, and designing this way for the rest of your career

The humility that vulnerability requires is also demonstrated by a willingness to admit the old ways we used to design were not only ineffective but also harmful. This gets to the "why" behind your shift to designing with cultural competence in the first place. If there is a lack of understanding around this point, there will surely be a reversion to old, comfortable practices. We must acknowledge the harm caused by exclusion to illustrate why inclusion is so necessary. To fully digest this, revisit past projects that could have been conducted differently or instances of internal pushback that were ignored or actively silenced or refer to the stories of design gone wrong presented in this book. Take the time to really reflect on the damage those approaches inflicted and make your own decisions about what you will no longer tolerate.

It will be just as significant to decide you are willing to adopt and model new behaviors in the design process. It's one thing to declare a shift to culturally competent design, but following that up with action is a whole different matter. That action must stem from a genuine, deliberate decision made from a place of humility. It must come from a desire to try new methods, practices, and activities that will yield solutions that authentically reflect humanity. When individuals within a design firm have made this decision, you'll see project managers re-evaluating in-progress projects and collaborating with designers to see how they can pivot. You'll see leaders strategizing about iterative approaches to evolving practices, policies, and procedures to ensure consistency in the customer experience, as well as the employee experience. And at the most fundamental level, you'll see a workforce of designers engaging in new, uncomfortable conversations for the ultimate good of customers.

None of these changes will happen unless there is a collective acceptance of discomfort. Change causes discomfort. Feeling vulnerable causes discomfort. Not having all the answers causes discomfort. Conversations about topics related to cultural identity and difference cause discomfort. But avoiding that discomfort is what has kept us in the damaging holding pattern we're in. That avoidance has stunted the evolution of the design practice for centuries. It's time to open our mouths as well as our minds to get to the growth on the other side of that discomfort.

Another essential step in the evolution of the design practice and in our own evolution as designers is the acknowledgement that there is no such thing as a one-size-fits-all design solution. There is no such thing as cutting corners in culturally competent design. Instead, you have to be willing to explore cultural identity for each and every design project, even if you have worked with a particular community on a project in the past. Cultural competence is about understanding and appreciating nuance and complexities among people of various backgrounds. With that appreciation comes an intentional and curious exploration that respects difference. It doesn't seek shortcuts or limit understanding to the designer's individual frame of reference or comfort zone. A culturally competent designer will demonstrate this mindset by committing the time to incorporate these activities into their process. That designer will express an openness to learn and to use their inherent gift of creativity to translate new knowledge into design solutions that honor the fullest range and depth of identities.

Just as designers embrace the endlessness of our creativity, we must be endlessly curious about the people we design for. We must operate from a place of knowing there is no possible way for any one person to comprehend the fullness of all humanity. That's the advantage of working with people from different backgrounds. By bringing them and their voices and experiences into the design process, we gain access to that many more perspectives. And not only do they bring their distinct knowledge, but they also bring new questions and contexts into the process.

Accordingly, a culturally competent designer who has embraced this concept builds a diverse designer network and strives to learn as much as they can about people and cultures, both inside and outside of their work environment. In addition to keeping up with design trends, they stay on top of societal and demographic shifts impacting their customers. A culturally competent designer comprehends the fluidity of the users we serve and is excited by the new territory we have yet to explore in our profession by broadening our scope on who those users are.

At the end of the day, that's what this mindset shift is about: adopting culturally competent design to ensure our profession stays current with the ways our world is evolving. For creatives, that's not a burden — it's a gift. It gives you that much more inspiration to tap into and that much more potential for your craft to expand and serve the breadth of humanity. Ultimately, by making this shift, you are recommitting to your profession — this time with humanity front and center — and you're opening up the doors to transform not only your career but also the way the people you serve experience the world and see themselves in it.

BOOST YOUR CULTURE QUOTIENT

You will know a culturally competent mindset shift is happening when questions come up, like how and where to start and how you'll know as a team that you're getting it right. There will likely be way more questions than answers at the beginning, but that will be an indicator that a new dialogue is opening up. Use those opportunities to start talking through ideas and putting the culturally competent habits in Chapter 3 to work. This type of transformation is fertile ground for the creativity designers bring to the table. Frame it as an opportunity to redesign your design philosophy and model inclusion and centering humanity in the process by inviting input.

The Environment Shift

When the mindset shift to designing with cultural competence happens, the environment can soon follow. New ways of thinking make space for new ways of engaging among your design teams and throughout your design firm. In essence, vulnerability, openness to designing differently, leading with curiosity, and willingness to learn contribute to a sense of psychological safety that gives people permission to embrace the ambiguity of venturing into this new, culturally aware territory and figure things out together.

This psychologically safe environment can be further reinforced by collectively agreeing to adopt and demonstrate certain behaviors as shown in Figure 7.

FIGURE 7—CULTURALLY COMPETENT
ENVIRONMENT SHIFT

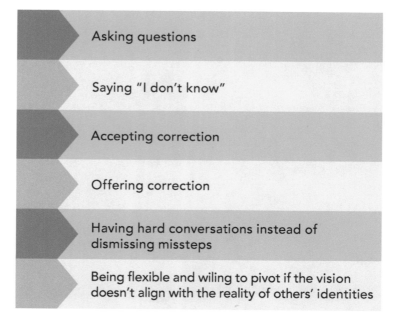

Asking questions

Saying "I don't know"

Accepting correction

Offering correction

Having hard conversations instead of dismissing missteps

Being flexible and wiling to pivot if the vision doesn't align with the reality of others' identities

While it will be critical to communicate the acceptance and expectation of these behaviors, it will be even more important for leaders and managers to demonstrate them. Their actions will signal that these are the new standards of behavior to be modeled across all levels of your organization.

An environment that fosters culturally competent design is one where questions about cultural identity are asked frequently, respectfully, and without retribution. Simply asking more questions throughout the design process creates space for new discussions that could result in more thoughtfully crafted solutions. To take it a step further, freely address-ing inquiries related to identity could also encourage designers with specific lived experience to contribute perspectives they may not have felt comfortable sharing in the past. A more open dialogue could signal to some team members that their insights are not only helpful but also truly valued. Imagine being a designer of a particular religious background, for example, with a wealth of information you're glad to share about your lifestyle, and finally feeling seen when you're invited to lend that expertise on a related project. Think about how much more included you would feel and how much higher the chances that you'd be forthcoming in the future.

Equally important to asking questions is creating an environment where designers can be transparent and openly admit "I don't know" when a matter around identity arises that they're not familiar with. Since we've established that no one individual can possibly comprehend the full scope and depth of humanity, it's critical that designers know it's acceptable to not have all the answers. Designers must be encouraged to explore and find those answers. Being able to say "I don't know" doesn't let a designer off the hook, but it can prevent them from making something up based on assumptions out of a fear of reprisal. It can also make space for conversations and possible collaboration to find the answers necessary to make informed design decisions.

As we're all navigating this territory of exploring cultural identity and finding the answers, we have to be prepared for the possibility that we may still get some things wrong. We may not even always get the questions themselves right. But a psychologically safe environment is one where corrections can be made respectfully and received and considered thoughtfully. A culturally competent design process includes multiple opportunities to engage with customers to identify and confirm critical details for the design solution. These instances aren't just checkpoints to prove that you, the designer, are correct. They are intentionally created opportunities to receive guidance and, if necessary, course correction in case you may have been misinformed or you have misinterpreted something meaningful to the users. In those moments, it's critical to receive feedback with an open mind and to be willing to adjust based on the knowledge offered to you.

It may also be the case that you spot an error or a questionable decision made by a colleague during the design process. As a culturally competent designer, it is your responsibility to raise that concern and hold your colleague responsible for correcting it or investigating further. In this new environment, the objective is to offer the correction in a way that allows it to be received, understood, and acted upon in a timely manner. With that in mind, it may be worthwhile to offer correction with an alternative solution or a recommendation for identifying one, such as pointing that person to credible resources.

BOOST YOUR CULTURE QUOTIENT

Establishing an environment where both offering and receiving correction are the norm can be a game changer in opening lines of communication. It may not be the easiest thing in the world, but it's also not impossible if enough people are willing to give it a shot. If you are the person who would like to raise an objection or concern, you have several options for doing so. If you have an established relationship with the individual who needs to be addressed, it may simply be a matter of approaching them one on one and saying, "Something that came up earlier isn't sitting right with me, and I'd like to run it by you." If you're further removed from the individual, you could bring it up in a similar way through a mutual contact or escalate it to someone who may have more direct influence in the situation.

If you are on the receiving end of a concern or correction, your most effective response will be: "Tell me more." It gives you an opportunity to get more information before you respond and signals that you're open to another perspective. That one gesture can defuse what could have been an awkward moment for both people involved in the dialogue. The most important point, however, is to be willing to listen and remain open to an exchange of viewpoints to arrive at a resolution, even if it's one that requires shifting course.

The Behavior Shift

This new psychologically safe environment makes space for new behaviors to emerge among your workforce. Once there is a perceived permission and expectation to consciously incorporate cultural identity into the design process and design solutions, your firm will realize the value and richness cultural competence brings to your work and your customers. New habits that once seemed burdensome will become routine. New approaches to everything from recruiting and retention to research and sourcing will become second nature. Because once you see design through a culturally competent lens, there's no way to go back to black and white.

Figure 8 lists a few indicators that your firm has made the behavior shift to designing with cultural competence.

FIGURE 8—CULTURALLY COMPETENT BEHAVIOR SHIFT

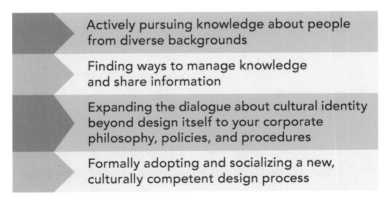

Actively pursuing knowledge about people from diverse backgrounds

Finding ways to manage knowledge and share information

Expanding the dialogue about cultural identity beyond design itself to your corporate philosophy, policies, and procedures

Formally adopting and socializing a new, culturally competent design process

Once the blinders come off and you see how other people's identities shape their lives, there's no denying its importance in the practice of design. The uncovering of this new dimension and your own mastery of folding this critical element into your work as an individual and as an organization sparks a natural desire to do more. Anxiety about saying and doing the right things is outweighed by the satisfaction of creating something that resonates with customers in a profoundly meaningful way. Worry about uncomfortable conversations is replaced with an unquenchable curiosity about the many opportunities to create more impactful designs you may have missed in the past.

At this point, designing with cultural competence no longer feels like a chore; it feels imperative. Accordingly, your staff requests new resources to expand their knowledge. They request to invite new speakers to educate your staff about socioeconomic trends that are changing the profile of your typical interior design client. They request to attend conferences on new advances in accessibility for online platforms. They start consulting with internal affinity groups to strategize ways to connect with and support causes relevant to your industry. They genuinely want to learn more about people and how they can tailor their craft accordingly to be more effective design professionals. And they expect their leadership will fully support such growth.

With the immense amount of knowledge being cultivated through culturally competent practices, there will be a great demand to make that information available and shareable for everyone to access. In the world we live in, data is the most valuable currency. As an organization, it would be a great disservice to gather valuable artifacts and case studies through one project or department that would not then be made available to others. A culturally competent design firm will factor this into their overall knowledge management strategy and identify ways this can be addressed in their organization.

Equally important to cataloging information is creating opportunities to actively share it. A culturally competent workforce will have an appreciation for the professional and personal experiences of their colleagues. And one of the best ways to convey those experiences is through storytelling. Centering the humanity of sharing very human experiences creates space for a different level of connection and exploration that can feed your creativity as a designer and your curiosity as a member of our collective society.

This new awareness and appreciation for the diversity of humanity doesn't just stop at client work and design. A culturally competent perspective also makes you start looking at your colleagues and your organization through new eyes. If acceptance and appreciation for identity can change the game for your customers, they can do the same for the people you work with day in and day out. Acknowledging your employees' identity can free up the energy they typically expend to downplay it. Examining the identities among your talent pool could help you tailor your recruiting approaches and improve your outcomes. Assessing your internal demographics, pay studies, performance ratings, promotion rates, and retention efforts could help you understand your workforce's perception of the value you truly place on diversity.

Designing with cultural competence will naturally transcend to living with cultural competence, and that will trigger a re-evaluation of how your organization shows up in the world. Your willingness to dive into that exercise and potentially adapt based on the resulting revelations will be just as critical as embracing cultural competence in the first place. If you claim to embrace humanity, you cannot subsequently pick and choose to do so only when it's convenient. There should be an expectation that this shift will set off a chain reaction that demands consistency for all stakeholders, both external and internal. And just as this shift opens the door for creativity and opportunity in design, it also opens the door for creativity and opportunity in management.

One of the most critical ways this new creativity manifests is in the formal organization-wide adoption and socialization of a new, culturally competent design process. Tying this back to the behavioral shift, this adoption has to take place in more than words alone. This goes beyond unspoken norms and loose interpretations of a design philosophy; this is about a whole new way of being. It must be aligned to and incorporated into the organization's mission, vision, and values. It must be articulated by leadership and managers. It must be a part of pitches and proposals. It must be stated in such a way that the entire workforce can grasp it and speak to it. It must be so clearly understood that new employees can pick it up with ease and potential clients can clearly distinguish what makes your process unique compared to the standard design approach. This is where your organization emerges as a beacon in the design landscape and a future-proof model for the design industry as a whole.

A shift to cultural competence is no small undertaking. It may require skills and behaviors that are not familiar to you or are completely out of the norm for your organization. Keep in mind that this is a significant transformation that will take time and consistent, concerted effort. It will be important to establish and communicate a vision, milestones, and indicators for growth. If you struggle in this area, it may be worthwhile to consult with a DEIB expert familiar with how embedding DEIB values translates into new culturally competent operational practices.

The most pivotal component of this behavior shift, in terms of day-to-day design practice, is the implementation of a culturally competent design process. In Chapter 5, we'll explore how an evolved mindset, environment, and behaviors bring new perspectives to light and result in design solutions that incorporate identity.

Scan this QR code to download a **discussion guide** for this chapter.

5

THE DESIGN
FOR IDENTITY
BLUEPRINT

The culturally competent design process is not actually a brand-new process. It's simply a new, human-centered iteration of the process most designers are familiar with and regularly use. The steps are the same. There are just new questions to ask.

Figure 9 depicts a standard design process comprised of eight basic phases:

1. **Understand:** Clarify requirements, timeline, and budget. Confirm the client's objectives and scope.

2. **Empathize:** Engage with the customer community to validate their requirements and needs.

3. **Define:** Clearly articulate the design concept.

4. **Ideate:** Brainstorm solutions; design.

5. **Prototype:** Craft solutions.

6. **Test:** Gather customer feedback on proposed solutions, incorporate feedback, iterate as needed, and arrive at an optimal solution.

7. **Produce:** Build and launch the selected solution.

8. **Improve:** Revisit the solution with customers to ensure continued fulfillment of objectives over time.

FIGURE 9—DESIGN PROCESS

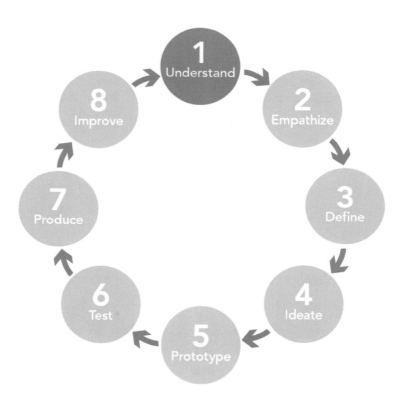

When we overlay this process with the cultural competence lens, we get the Design for Identity Blueprint. This blueprint specifies what to ask, who to ask, and when during the design process to ensure that factors critical to the customers' identity are not an afterthought. It incorporates new questions into several critical phases: Empathize, Define, Ideate, Prototype, Test, and Improve.

FIGURE 10—THE DESIGN FOR IDENTITY BLUEPRINT

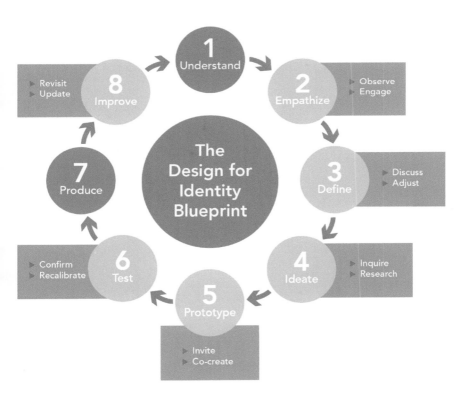

Applying the Design for Identity Blueprint introduces new facets that require coordination among the design team, as well as interaction with customers during these phases.

BOOST YOUR
CULTURE QUOTIENT

Perspectives from a Designer

Name: Jan Baker

Occupation: Experience and Service Designer

Q: How do you describe your role in design?

A: My role as an experience and service designer is to help organizations design services, experiences, and products that don't leave anyone out and have cultural relevance at the forefront by melding the digital with the physical. It's hard to describe the absence of the intangible; however, it is something that you feel immensely, and you identify it immediately when it is there. It makes you feel good. That's a mouthful, however, no longer do we live in a world that is insular. Experiences, reviews, and technology drive everything that we do. If a customer or end user does not feel good, they have a voice that can and will be heard. The delivery of services, programs, products, and experiences is emotional, and I focus on the intentionality and attention to detail to create an appealing, inclusive memory that keeps customers coming back.

Q: What effective methods have you used in service design to gain insights into users' cultural identities?

A: I have an advantage when it comes to sensitivity of cultural identities. As a Black person, woman, immigrant, and having had a disability over multiple times of my life, I design with a certain level of empathy, compassion, awareness, and curiosity. By experience and journey mapping, identifying where technology fits and/or human interaction is preferable, and using design thinking, I work to create memorable engagements with the digital and physical. At one point in my career, I worked for a billion-dollar organization that focused on women customers between the ages of forty-five and sixty-five. The company was going through a digital revolution, and the traditional line of business (selling products on TV) was being cannibalized by digital sales. The target customer was also different on the digital side. The tech team was almost exclusively men who built tech products that were shiny and did cool things. They didn't ask women what they wanted or even talk to the customer service team. Apps were created in a vacuum until I empowered the few women on the team to speak up. I led a session with the men on the team who didn't realize they were excluding the women and worked with the customer experience team to create a feedback loop between the app developers, creative team, and customer experience team. We also created an in-app chat feature that extracted comments and data for real-time feedback. The business grew, communication was better, everyone on the team felt included, and we received positive feedback from customers. The digital side went on to sixty percent of the business that was thirty-five years old at that time.

Q: In what ways do you think service design could be transformed to incorporate cultural identity?

A: Many services (experiences and products) were designed from a white point of view or intended for white people. It's just the way that it is. If services were more inclusive, there would not be so many apologies that need to be issued. It literally starts with the notion of accomplices and not allies — those who are willing to risk something to ensure that diversity and representation are at the helm. This can only happen with the extraction of ego.

Nothing is really hard when it comes to user research and also needing those participants to find the points within the service that are exclusionary and actually listening to those people on why these elements are important. Finding those pain points *before* the service launches creates less need for apologies and rework. Customers know when cultural identity was an afterthought.

Take Rihanna's Fenty Beauty, for example. For such a long time, customers were begging for more inclusive color-ways. Rihanna merely designed for herself and created a spectrum of makeup products that included those lacking pigmentation with albinism to those who come from Sudan and have the darkest skin on the planet, the Nilotes. After the success of Fenty Beauty and the perfect blend of in-person with digital technology, she captured the market. It was then that the main players reacted and broadened their offerings. This was too late for a customer like me. This is also why Rihanna became a billionaire.

It's simple: Just design for everyone and make the effort. My company aims to design for various industries and revolutionize like Rihanna did for makeup and clothing. Inclusivity should cease to be "a thing" and become a part of lifestyle.

Design for Identity Blueprint: **Empathize**

This phase is critical to establishing a connection with the user community to ensure authentic representation of cultural identity in the final product your team designs. This is where you immerse yourself in the users' world to gain insight into their lifestyles, routines, and habits to validate the requirements established at the outset of the project. It's critical to begin exploring the topic of identity at this point to set the tone and direction for the project. Starting here ensures key factors won't be treated as afterthoughts; instead, they will be baked in right from the beginning.

This is where your meaningful engagement with the users begins. In order to really see them and gather cultural clues that will make the end product resonate with them, you really have to get informed about who they are, how they view themselves, and what aspects of their identity are most relevant in the context of what you're creating for them. This is where you observe dynamics, note any traditions or rituals, and hone in on what's prevalent in their spaces, their discussions, and even their attire. Both tangible and intangible factors come into play.

What might you observe? Let's take the example of redesigning a community center. At this phase, you would want to know the demographics of the surrounding community, including race, ethnicity, socioeconomic status, age, professions, and other factors. But more importantly, you would want to know who uses the existing center, in what ways, why, and why not. You may conduct interviews with staff and community members or spend some time there, watching what people typically do in the space, how much time they spend there, and who they interact with.

While you may make significant surface observations, there could be game-changing nuances you miss if you fail to explicitly inquire about cultural identity. For instance, you may note a significant senior population utilizes the center. If the surrounding culture is one where seniors are typically well cared for in multigenerational households, it might be the case that they use the center as more of a peer gathering place than a meal distribution center, for example, which will dictate the uses for space inside. If there are dominant religions in the community, it may be worthwhile to find out what services are provided by local houses of worship, so the center's offerings can complement or augment them, if necessary, and not duplicate them. This information could also dictate what symbology is most appropriate to incorporate into the space.

The surrounding area could also be one that is diversifying, and long-time residents may be fearful of their history getting lost in the dialogue. That could be a clue to inquire about the legacy of the old neighborhood and how that could be represented in the updated space, possibly through imagery or function. These meaningful details are uncovered by deliberately asking people what about their identity they would like to see reflected in the final product.

As a design team, you have to be geared up to explore these aspects. For one thing, you have to have the awareness that people are multidimensional and that you need to rely on more than your frame of reference — what you think you see, hear, and observe — to get a complete picture of who you're designing for. This is where cultural competence comes into play. A diverse group of observers will yield more dynamic perspectives of the people you observe. Therefore, it's valuable to have individuals with varied lived experiences on your team, so they can share observations and raise questions based on a broader scope of understanding. This is the lens that cultural competence brings to this phase of the design process.

But there's more to it than just having diversity on your team. The next and most critical step is really knowing your team. Understand their backgrounds, what aspects of identity resonate with them, and what cultural indicators they look for and where. Get to know what types of conversations they are skilled at and equipped to engage in to surface the information that's truly going to respectfully fold the users' culture into the design. The awareness and perspective of the observer are as critical as the observing itself. With all these insights on the table, you can determine who is best prepared to gather the observations you need at this point to move the project forward.

I want to reiterate here that applying the cultural competence lens isn't about revamping the entire design process. It disrupts without interrupting. It transforms the norm into something more extraordinary. In this phase, it simply introduces new perspectives to the standard fact-finding activities that commonly leave out cultural identity. The ability to do this relies heavily on establishing the mindset, behaviors, and environment detailed in the previous chapter. This is how you ensure the right conversations are had, the right individuals are a part of this phase of the design process, and cultural identity is accounted for. With all these elements in place, you can really start thinking about the questions you must ask in order to make this phase as thorough as possible. Some of those questions will need to be addressed among your design team, and others will need to be directed to your customers. They are all summarized in Table 1.

Your design team will have to engage in a dialogue about who the right observers are to bring in at this phase. This moment calls for intentional, direct discussion about what you know about the identities of your customers as well as the identities, experience, and expertise of your team members to maximize the potential for picking up on relevant culture clues. Keep in mind that they may be existing project team members or others from different areas of your organization. These observers will have to be the right people for the task. They should have not only cultural awareness but also emotional intelligence and communication skills to effectively engage with the customers.

Once selected, these observers will have to strategize about which customers to engage and the most appropriate ways to interface with them to get the insights they need. In the community center example, they may choose to visit for a day or drop in on regularly scheduled activities for casual conversations. They may speak with staff, current visitors, and various members of the community. After figuring out the how, they will also have to determine what types of insights would be most helpful based on the stated objectives of the project. They should have a standard format for capturing and presenting their findings, so the information is digestible and accessible to the entire team for the remainder of the project lifecycle.

To be most effective, the observers will have to agree on what indicators they're looking for and which are most critical for determining the requirements for your project. In addition to what they pick up on visually and audibly, they should explicitly inquire about which elements of their cultural identity the users would like to see celebrated in the space/product/item you're designing. They should also take this opportunity to ask customers themselves if there are other sources they should speak to and any other perspectives they should seek out to get a better understanding of the cultural aspects of the project. After all, customers are the experts on themselves. Getting this information straight from the source minimizes the chances of making inaccurate assumptions that result in performative or misguided design.

With all this information in hand, your team will be ready to enter the define phase where you will translate and distill your findings into culturally relevant design requirements.

TABLE 1—DESIGN FOR IDENTITY BLUEPRINT
QUESTIONS: EMPATHIZE

Questions for the Design Team	Questions for the Customers
Whose perspectives do we need to accurately validate the customers' needs?	What about your identity or cultural background would you like to be celebrated in this space/item/product?
What are the best ways to engage with these customers? (e.g., observation, interviews, etc.)	Whose perspectives do we need to accurately identify your needs and those of others who may be impacted by this design?
What type of insights will be most helpful for this type of project?	What are the best ways to get the information we need to properly complete this project?
Who among our team is best equipped and informed to engage authentically and effectively with these customers?	Are there any other perspectives we should consider?

BOOST YOUR CULTURE QUOTIENT

How do you select the most appropriate observers? The best observers will have relevant lived experience and be skilled at discussing cultural identity. Note: This is not a default role for the person who's most passionate about DEIB or the member of an underrepresented group who has been tokenized in your organization. There should be dialogue happening to allow people to express interest, and then they should be vetted for the appropriate skills. If you don't have the expertise in house, consider bringing in a DEIB expert for their services or recommendations on how to proceed.

Design for Identity Blueprint: **Define**

At this point in the design process, you have defined parameters from your client and valuable insights from the customers to help inform your design concept. You are ready to articulate your vision for the final product with a fair degree of confidence in its alignment with their needs. And because you have already started a dialogue about cultural identity, your concept includes some of those aspects as well.

A culturally competent design team will have two major checkpoints in this phase. They'll have one among themselves, in the process of developing the concept, and another when validating the concept with the customers. The first discussion is where you assess the cultural findings you gathered in the emphathize phase and their implications for the design. You note the recurring themes or commonly mentioned elements across the multiple channels you used to engage with the customers and settle on which to weave into your vision for the end product. You are not necessarily at the point of figuring out how those elements and themes will be translated into design features yet. You just need to be able to state what they are, so they can be confirmed with the customers.

In our community center example, this may be where your team determines that what's most significant to the community is preserving their legacy while simultaneously embracing the increasing diversity in the area. Let's say that it's a predominantly Black neighborhood where residents' families go back several decades, many living in homes passed down from generation to generation. They have fond memories of some family-owned stores that recently went out of business, and many of the neighbors are members of the same church. There are a few hometown heroes from the community who have played pivotal roles at the local and national levels. This rich history could be incorporated into the design concept and explicitly folded into the narrative of the vision your team presents to both the clients and the community. In doing so, you will show your commitment to making them feel heard and that you respect their story and who they are. This will go a long way in differentiating your firm from others that just check the box and produce trendy, self-serving designs driven only by pleasing the client and your own creative whims. It will also reinforce the sentiment of cooperation and respect within the community and position them to thrive together moving into the future with this center as a living monument to those ideals.

The next step is to present the concept to see how it resonates with your customers. This is another key dialogue in which your team deliberately asks whether you have hit the mark in terms of emphasizing and incorporating aspects of their identity that are most meaningful to them. This would also be where you ask if there's anything you've left out that should be considered and whether there are specific features to avoid in the final design. For our fictitious community center, it may turn out that some of the proclaimed neighborhood heroes have controversial pasts, so it may be best not to highlight them in either name or imagery in the final design. Or the storied local church may want to downplay their representation at the community center to allow for a more welcoming environment for new neighbors of other faiths. This is the type of input that's not only important to gather but useful to know before design truly gets underway in the ideate phase.

TABLE 2—DESIGN FOR IDENTITY BLUEPRINT
QUESTIONS: DEFINE

Questions for the Design Team	Questions for the Customers
Have we effectively identified which cultural aspects to incorporate into the design? What else do we need to know to authentically represent these features in our design?	Have we accurately identified which cultural aspects to incorporate into the design? Are there certain aspects we should prioritize or emphasize over others? Are there any symbols, motifs, images, verbiage, or colors we should avoid?

Design for Identity Blueprint: Ideate

This is where your creativity really takes flight as you expand on your design concept and give form to ideas. In this phase, you explore how your concept can translate into a space, an object, or an experience. You get to flex your skills of creation, and as a culturally competent designer, you examine how to interpret cultural concepts you uncovered in previous phases and incorporate them into the overall design.

This is a pivotal phase for the culturally competent designer because the intel you gathered is only valuable if it makes it into the final product, and this is where you begin figuring out what that looks like. This may be a new kind of challenge, but designers are problem solvers if nothing else. So looking through the lens of cultural competence, you should just see this as another facet to explore in creating a truly whole design. Once again, the ideate tasks are still the same. There's just a new dimension to incorporate, and there are new types of resources to turn to for inspiration.

Your team would typically look through archives to make sure they were creating something new and original or maybe converse with colleagues about similar approaches by the experts in your discipline. In the same way, you'll need to identify sources that inform cultural representation. In those conversations, you will raise a question about what relevant resources your team has access to that would be helpful to consult and who within your organization, network, or profession can provide input and/or recommendations. This step will likely require research, and possibly brainstorming, to identify the proper references.

Consider your customers as a resource, too. Keep in mind you are the expert on design, but they are the experts on themselves. While they are not required to do the work for you — nor should they be treated that way — they just might be able to refer you to some valuable sources. They could also help you confirm the validity of the resources you are referencing.

Let's go back to our community center project. Your team may have done some research and come across images of old storefronts, names of local figures the community collectively would like to honor, and popular vendors who typically sell goods at regular community activities, like block parties. You may have also learned the community would like to celebrate the heritage of its newcomers as well, and they envision the revamped center as a place where they can learn about and from one another. These elements could translate into the naming of spaces within the center, the functions and features of those spaces, imagery, color schemes, and more. Learning about the respected makers in the area could also present opportunities for outreach and collaboration, so they could contribute to the design in some way. This would be the phase where your team begins the dialogue about specific features that are meaningful to the community to inform what will show up in the final design.

TABLE 3—DESIGN FOR IDENTITY BLUEPRINT
QUESTIONS: IDEATE

Questions for the Design Team	Questions for the Customers
What resources do we have access to that would help us in our research? Who among our team might be willing and able to provide some relevant perspectives and input?	Are we on the right path? Are there resources you would recommend for us to more fully understand the cultural aspects of this project? Are there any instances you could share where this has been achieved to your satisfaction?

BOOST YOUR CULTURE QUOTIENT

The method you use to execute this step is as critical as the information you are attempting to gather. Do not approach the one woman, Black person, brown person, older person, gay person, or otherwise "representative" person in your organization and put them in a position to provide guidance just because their identity appears to align with that of the customers you're designing for. The term for that is tokenism. It's prejudicial, damaging, and violating and does not align with the culturally competent mindset, behaviors, or environment described in this book. Those individuals are not obligated or equipped to speak on behalf of an entire demographic. Consider instead putting out an open call for insights relevant to the cultural context you're exploring, and provide flexible options for people to respond, anonymously or otherwise. Or ask if anyone can recommend resources your team can consult.

BOOST **YOUR** CULTURE QUOTIENT

Perspectives from a Designer

Name: Rebecca Sistruck

Occupation: Workplace Strategist & Change Practitioner

Q: How do you describe your role in design?

A: My focus and expertise within the corporate design industry is developing workplace strategies that influence the human experience in a positive way. I look for ways to engage the lived experience and incorporate inclusivity in the early stages of strategic planning. I believe design begins with understanding that people are at the center of a "designed" built environment. Thoughtful inquiry and research influence a strategic approach to planning and design.

Q: In what instances do you see designers' identities addressed in design practice?

A: Historically in workplace design and strategy, I have seen very few diverse identities deliberately represented in the design team creation or within the clients' teams. However, in civic, community, and school project types (K-12 and higher ed), I have been included in project teams/pursuits for the optics versus my expertise. Due to the selection process and potential diverse nature of the institutions, clients are looking for a more diverse experience and expertise in their architecture and design teams.

Q: What do you think interior design firms could do better to incorporate cultural identity into spaces?

A: I believe there are four key areas that should be prioritized:

1. Internal cultural shift in the structure of architecture and design firms to remove traditional hierarchy. This includes stronger people-focused leadership/management and building stronger community connections to better understand lived experience of others.

2. Evaluation of how firms can diversify workforce through thorough assessment of hiring strategies.

3. Expand awareness of the profession among people of color. This will improve and build a stronger pipeline.

4. Expand business development efforts to focus on diverse clients. This will facilitate more discussion about both client and community experiences.

Design for Identity Blueprint: **Prototype**

With the ideate phase complete, the actual creation begins in the prototype phase. As a culturally competent design team, you have even more inspiration than you may have had otherwise because you've taken a lot of guesswork out of the process. You're not just aiming in the dark, trying to come up with something new and innovative. You're not just guided and restricted by a list of basic, impersonal requirements provided by a client who will likely never really use what you're designing. You have input directly from the people you are designing for, which will help you and your team create something that will speak to them in truly significant ways.

Out of respect for those same people, this phase also incorporates a couple of intentional checkpoints to make sure their voice is honored in this process. Once again, your design expertise is not in question here. This is a matter of validating that they can still see their input incorporated into the design and seeking a diverse range of perspectives before the design is considered complete. At this point, you're conducting cultural competence quality control to avoid corrections or omissions that would cost considerable time, funds, and resources further down the road.

Among your team, you're keeping the cultural elements top of mind in the discussions and assessments of the overall design. You're taking into account the perspectives of teammates, and you're also consciously seeking input from colleagues of different backgrounds. You're not looking for a critique but a range of impressions about what the design conveys from a cultural standpoint. You want to know what resonates and what seems misaligned, what seems trite and what seems more nuanced. That feedback is then combined with similar insights gathered from the customers. The goal is the same with customers — to seek perspectives from as diverse a pool of people as possible. Involving them also gives you an opportunity to confirm whether your solution meets their needs and expectations, which is ultimately what applying the cultural competence lens is about.

A critical point to keep in mind here is that interactions at this phase aren't just about asking questions; they're more about getting answers. And you have to be ready and willing to make adjustments based on the responses you receive. Authentic engagement requires the humility to accept correction or redirection to ensure the final product is just as much about the customers' identity as it is about your savvy and expertise. You may have to go back and forth to get the details right, but that time is well spent if it averts trivializing, diminishing, or harming people you engaged as partners earlier in the design process.

This would be the point in the community center project where you demonstrate how and where you incorporated the names and imagery you proposed in the ideate phase and ensure that you've used them appropriately. The prototype phase is your opportunity to co-create significant cultural moments in the space with the community you're designing for. For example, there may be a preference to more prominently feature photos of a bakery owned by a beloved neighbor as opposed to the old corner store, or there might be a desire to create more flexible display systems in one area to allow for rotating recognition of different cultural observances and local events. Perhaps neighbors were able to connect with local preservationists further along in the process who they would like to have weigh in on the design. This is where you invite the customers' participation in a way that transforms identity into reality.

TABLE 4—DESIGN FOR IDENTITY BLUEPRINT
QUESTIONS: PROTOTYPE

Questions for the Design Team	Questions for the Customers
Who should we invite to provide feedback on the prototype?	Have we invited the proper stakeholders into this phase of the process?
Are there any perspectives we're missing?	Are there any perspectives we're missing?
	Do these solutions meet your expectations?
	What improvements could we make?

Design for Identity Blueprint: **Test**

If you have designed with cultural competence up to this point, any feedback you receive in the test phase should involve minor tweaks or suggestions for future consideration or iteration. Your team and your customers should be able to look at the final product and see the customers represented in it.

The design should do all of the following:

- ▶ Honor and celebrate the identity of the customers
- ▶ Cause no sense of harm, disrespect, or erasure
- ▶ Embody the spirit of the customers' needs and expectations
- ▶ Reflect the expressed values of the customers as conveyed throughout the design process

As a culturally competent designer, you'll explicitly seek this type of feedback in your customer's evaluation of the product you created. You'll also record any recommendations for the improve phase and document your successful practices, impactful solutions, and useful resources as reference points for future projects.

At the close of the community center project, this phase would likely include an amended post-occupancy evaluation that delves into customers' cultural experience of the space in addition to their physical experience of it. Beyond their assessment of the form and function of the design, customers would weigh in on the points specified above. They'd also have an opportunity to provide you with insights for future updates that would make the center that much more culturally resonant.

After all the feedback sessions and discussions, there's still nothing like living and existing in a space. That's how the customers really get to see if the environment suits their needs. And that's when they get a real sense of what cultural signals are truly reinforced through the design choices that were made. Do they translate from one neighbor to the next? Has the history been highlighted without alienating newcomers? These indicators of culturally competent design can only be measured after customers' exposure and with their direct input.

TABLE 5—DESIGN FOR IDENTITY BLUEPRINT
QUESTIONS: TEST

Question for the Design Team	Question for the Customers
Does our solution align with the needs expressed by our customers?	Does our solution align with your needs and expectations?

BOOST YOUR
CULTURE QUOTIENT

Perspectives from a Designer

Name: Tama Duffy Day, FACHE, FASID, FIIDA, LEED AP

Occupation: Principal and Co-Leader of Gensler's global design practice focused on health

Q: How do you describe your role in design?

A: I am a strategist, creating a better world through the power of design. Gensler is a global architecture, design, and planning firm.

Q: What's one critical practice interior designers could adopt to get design right for special populations, such as older adults?

A: We are living in an unprecedented time where the population aged sixty-five and over is growing faster than all other age groups — and this is happening on a global scale. According to data from the UN's 2022 Revision of World Population Prospects, by 2050, sixteen percent of the global population will be over age sixty-five, an increase from ten percent in 2022. Right now, we need to focus on age-inclusive design that takes into account vision, hearing, balance, memory, touch, and more. It should be a concern for all of society because when we design for the oldest and youngest generations, everyone ultimately benefits. With this in mind, every industry should seek to entice, delight, and design for the new aging consumer.

Q: What changes are you seeing in design practice that are creating more space for cultural identity in the dialogue?

A: Equity has to be a prime consideration for all entrepre- neurs and businesses, especially those businesses focused on health. Disproportionately negative health outcomes for people of color have persisted throughout the history of the United States, and the pandemic only served to worsen them and put a spotlight on the problem. I can't imagine a design solution that doesn't involve a focus on community and population health. We just can't move forward without widening our scope. As cities seek to address systemic injustice, they'll have to take a hard look at how their healthcare systems often perpetuate that injustice — and how they could alleviate it instead. We are excited that many of our clients agree and this strategic direction is in motion.

Design for Identity Blueprint: **Improve**

Change is a constant we can always count on. Design changes, culture shifts, needs evolve, and so do people. So a solution you create today will need to adapt over time to maintain both its usefulness and its relevance. A culturally competent designer knows that elements related to identity will have to be re-evaluated when future phases or iterations of the original design are executed.

One great benefit of having applied the Design for Identity Blueprint in the test phase is that it will have yielded valuable feedback to give you a starting point for improvement. Prior application of the Design for Identity Blueprint will also have given you and your team the perspectives and practice to frame the conversation necessary to factor cultural evolution into your exploration of the evolved design. It will be natural to you to discuss among yourselves what societal shifts — on both a micro and macro level — have taken place that could influence the design. You will give thoughtful consideration to who to invite into the conversation within your firm and among your clients and customers, and past experience will have revealed to you some useful resources to consult prior to and in addition to engaging with the customers.

Another benefit of completing the original design with cultural competence is that you will have already established strong customer relationships in the process that will be useful in the improve phase. You will have identified relevant stakeholders and built trust and connections needed to confirm past feedback and explore new factors of relevance to them. You will also be able to ask them if there are new stakeholders who should be brought into the process. And considering that no project is without a defined scope, you can ask them what's most critical and urgent to address in this phase and what improvements will be most meaningful to them.

The improve phase of the community center project could involve revisiting post-occupancy evaluations and setting up informal focus groups with neighbors who contributed to the original design to discuss prior feedback and obtain new insights. You may find the age demographics in the neighborhood have shifted and younger families are seeking features that help their children understand the cultural backgrounds of the community. With the older population dwindling, there could be a desire to capture, honor, and display their stories through various media. There may be a push to incorporate multiple languages into signage to facilitate communication for a rapidly growing population from certain ethnicities. These types of inputs can go a long way in ensuring that identity remains a key component of the space. This degree of engagement also communicates to the community that you as designers see them as people and that you recognize that culture is not stagnant and design is not prescriptive. You know that improvement is not just about refreshing paint or upgrading technology. It's about the space continuing to mirror the people who occupy it.

TABLE 6—DESIGN FOR IDENTITY BLUEPRINT
QUESTIONS: IMPROVE

Questions for the Design Team	Questions for the Customers
What do we need to ask to ensure that the cultural aspects of our design solution still resonate with our customers?	What, if any, cultural, societal, political, or other changes should we address in the next iteration of this product?
What changes are we and our colleagues aware of that may impact this next design iteration of the solution?	What would be the best features to revisit? (e.g., verbiage, symbolism, etc.)
What degree of redesign is reasonable for the scope of this effort?	Given the established scope for this project, which changes do you think are most critical to address?
	Whose input should we seek to effectively address these changes?
	What would a successful outcome for this next iteration of the design look like to you?

The culturally competent design process is the natural next iteration of design for designers and firms that seek to embed the values of diversity, equity, inclusion, and belonging not only into their culture but in how they function as practitioners.

BOOST YOUR
CULTURE QUOTIENT

Perspectives from a Designer

Name: Melanie Charlton

Occupation: Founder & Chief Creative, Brllnt (Graphic Design & Design Thinking/Strategy)

Q: How do you describe your role in design?

A: My role is to understand business strategic goals and translate them into visual solutions that fulfill the needs of our users and audiences. I also mentor and guide my team, partners, and community members in their own design journeys as we all seek to create solutions that are more representative and sustainable and promote equity for all people, especially those who have been historically overlooked and undervalued.

Q: What is one critical factor designers should consider when designing with cultural competence?

A: To me, design thinking is a framework that encourages user-centricity, giving the opportunity to not only better understand individual needs, but also build solutions that are intended to be changed and updated to continue meeting a changing need set in the future. This is an especially important strategy given what we have learned from these years of COVID bringing so many rapid, unexpected changes across businesses. The rush to change photos to ones representing safety precautions early in the pandemic to today's push to represent locations as vibrant, thriving, and most likely mask-free is just one simple example of how a designer needs to keep an evolving need set in mind for their solution. In this case, enabling the client to easily change out images to align with conditions will have shown good foresight in meeting future needs that can be anticipated with the initial ask.

Q: What practices have you implemented in your own organization to create an environment where people freely share input based on their lived experience?

A: Creating space for conversation by modeling openness and vulnerability in my own life and experiences is one way I've approached building a culture of inclusiveness. Sharing my own stories opens me up to getting feedback from my team to see my own blind spots within my storytelling, as well as allowing them to observe how sharing vulnerable information might be received by the team. But creating a safe space for dialogue is only the start. The real test of an inclusive and listening culture is actually incorporating ideas, suggestions, and takeaways from the feedback we receive into our design solutions.

I don't remember the exact story, but a comment I made about imprisoned people sparked a former colleague to point out that I had a bias, which in turn shifted my perspective and enabled the work we did to design a micro- exhibit about mass incarceration for the ACLU. I wish I remembered the exact exchange to share, but I will never forget the effect of her words, as it has forever reframed how I think and speak about those who are or have been incarcerated.

Applying the Design for Identity Blueprint accomplishes the following:

- ▶ It celebrates diversity by actively seeking a range of perspectives from design colleagues and customers alike and demonstrates their value by respectfully folding them into the design solution

- ▶ It promotes equity by giving a voice to those who are being designed for, as well as those who are doing the designing

- ▶ It encourages inclusion through deliberate, authentic engagement and outreach

- ▶ It fosters belonging by creating moments and environments where new insights about identity are sought out and freely shared because of an expectation that they'll be received and appreciated

These practices yield experiences that enrich the act of designing and assign a new level of significance to being designed for. Culturally competent design is what our increasingly diverse marketplace needs. And it's what you, as a designer, need to practice to remove barriers that have stifled the cultural richness of what our industry can provide to the world.

Scan this QR code to download the **Design for Identity Blueprint questions** and a **discussion guide** for this chapter.

BOOST YOUR CULTURE QUOTIENT

Perspectives from a Designer

Name: Jazmyne Simmons

Occupation: Product and Interior Designer

Q: How do you describe your role in design?

A: I believe my role at its simplest is to use my talents to transcend design across spaces to bridge and empower others. I specialize in residential interiors, user experience, and business and design thinking. It's important to me that whatever I deliver is equally weighted in beauty, function, and inclusiveness. To me, this is achieved by considering the immediate and long-term effects of the designs, including how empowered a user feels to navigate or elevate beyond our time together.

Q: What's one critical skill you think designers must utilize in discussions with customers about cultural identity?

A: I believe that listening is one critical skill designers must utilize in conversations with customers of diverse backgrounds. Being vulnerable and open enough to mirror the words a client and/or customer is sharing helps set a caring and intentional tone that creates a comfortable and collaborative environment. Whether I identify with or relate to a person doesn't matter. How can I be open enough to approach each person with an abundance of curiosity to honor their diverse experiences? I believe keeping a curious mindset not only builds rapport and limits bias, but it allows for the opportunity to reach a better outcome that reflects the client. I've found the better I listen to clients, the faster and better a project turns out.

Q: In your experience, what conditions make it possible for customers to discuss their lived experience in a design setting?

A: In my experience, embracing and welcoming our unique-ness as designers makes it easier for customers to discuss their lived experiences. For example, my hair is curly and voluminous. Over the last several years, I've learned to untether myself from the unspoken Eurocentric profes-sional standards within interior design and allow my hair to take its big natural state. Despite all the microaggressions I've encountered, I believe my courage to live out my expe-riences allowed one of my clients of diverse backgrounds to open up comfortably about their children's hair as we discussed their bedrooms.

I've never seen or heard designers struggle to accept the uniqueness of pets when designing. We've learned to accept their differences and quirks and are accustomed to designing spaces that fit those needs. I want the same freedom of expression for us as people. We are all differ-ent and should be able to have a space tailored to us and our needs.

Q: What's one thing design firms could start doing right now to ensure that diverse identities and experiences are reflected in the products, spaces, and experiences they produce?

A: I believe design firms could accomplish this by taking inven-tory of the type of products or people they're serving every so often. Naturally, our work could mirror an audience with similar traits or personalities as the people within the firm. Whether it's bringing in DEI consultants, attending continuing education workshops, traveling, seeking communities of diverse backgrounds, or a combination of all four plus more, I think it's important that we continue to recognize that we as designers are inherently biased and need awareness to ensure we are dynamic to meet the evolving manifestations and interpretations of inclusivity within the world we live in.

6

CULTURALLY COMPETENT DESIGN AS ACTIVISM

When we heeded the call to become designers, we entered into multiple systems that historically placed one identity above others. These systems were consciously constructed to diminish people based on their race, ethnicity, gender, sexual orientation, age, class, religion, ability, and more. We stepped into an education system steeped in Western civilization that minimizes global diversity while wondering why there's still so little diversity in the classrooms. Then we joined businesses and corporations that seek to profit from customer bases they don't even bother to understand or serve in meaningful ways. We operate in a political and economic environment that still has a long way to go to convince people whose identities have long been ignored to trust that attempts to uplift them are not simply pandering or fleeting publicity stunts that will abruptly end after the next election cycle.

But just as we chose to enter these systems, we can choose to perpetuate them or disrupt them. We inherited them in their current form, but we must acknowledge that systems are upheld by individuals who enforce the rules and embody the behaviors necessary to keep them going. Cultural competence is what it's going to take to rewire our systems and empower ourselves and our fellow designers to broaden our view of humanity and celebrate the depth and breadth of diversity among us.

Consciously infusing cultural competence into the practice of design is a **revolutionary** act. And design itself can be, and historically has been, a revolutionary act. If we look at it literally, design has been used as a form of protest, whether in the creation of an iconic poster proclaiming "I Am A Man" used during the Poor People's Campaign in Washington, DC, during the summer of 1968, or the emerging iterations of Pride flags that seek to establish visibility for different segments of the LGBTQ community. In addition to what we design, how we choose to design, and how we use design are also means of protest. The Design for Identity Blueprint is one of the tools at your disposal.

Design can be a powerful tool for change, so it's not a far leap to make the case for design as activism, which is about taking action to make change. Activism differs from advocacy and allyship, which revolve around making your position against injustices known. Activism is about taking a stand, making yourself heard, shaking things up, and bringing about different outcomes on a grand scale. Activism results in new policies and norms that fundamentally change communities, systems, and, yes, even design firms and the design industry.

Revolutionize Your Design Firm to Better Serve Your Workforce

Norms in design can be changed to make space for diverse perspectives to be acknowledged. Within design firms, as in any organization, some of the most impactful change starts at the top. As a design leader, you can use your authority to make new decisions that challenge standard practices from recruiting and hiring to professional development. Here are a few ideas to implement to evolve your firm's ethos.

Recruit on a Global Level

The pandemic has expanded our appreciation for the efficiency and effectiveness of remote work. This way of work removes barriers to design talent around the world. These designers can bring new perspectives to your firm and how you design. Expand the scope of your search and simultaneously expand your mind to embrace the work of diverse talent that reflects their respective cultures. Be open to innovation through cross-cultural cross-pollination. Invite in what's new to you and see how much you and your workforce can learn.

Reassess Educational Background Requirements

Revisit your hiring policies to expand the desired educational background of candidates. Consider the value a background in sociology, anthropology, or ethnic studies could bring to your design process and to navigating topics related to culture and identity. Consider the value subject-matter expertise in change management and design thinking could add in the adoption of the Design for Identity Blueprint.

Hire Culture Facilitators

Hire culture facilitators in your firm. It's not uncommon for design firms to have sustainability experts or usability experts on staff. Why not culture experts? A culture facilitator is specially trained to engage with and listen to groups to impartially surface their often-unspoken norms, beliefs, challenges, and obstacles. A culture facilitator can unearth critical insights that can change the game when it comes to co-creating and designing with, as opposed to for, end users.

In organizations that lack this expertise, this role can be left to the more sociable "people person" on the team, the one who can build a quick rapport and guide a conversation. But social skills are not the same as facilitation skills. A facilitator can draw out and distill the type of qualitative data that makes the Design for Identity Blueprint most effective. A culturally competent design firm relies on these game changers because they can work with your clients to gather critical information your design staff needs to go from creators to collaborators.

Hire Designers with Cultural Expertise

Hire or contract with designers who specialize in designing for certain populations. Extend this thinking beyond those who design for the aging or for people with disabilities. Research successful projects for communities of specific ethnic or religious backgrounds or socioeconomic status, for example, and partner with the responsible designers to get their insights and expose your staff to their knowledge. Go out of your way to build up a network of culturally competent resources to partner with in your work.

Encourage Specialization in DEIB

Expand your in-house training offerings or broaden the scope of your existing training policies to cover DEIB. Incentivize staff to earn DEIB certifications. Create opportunities for these cross-trained professionals to teach the rest of your workforce through training the trainer, communities of practice, and learning circles. Or consider matrixing these professionals out as internal consultants across all your projects.

Sponsor Professional Development for Employees in Marginalized Groups

Sponsor professional association memberships for employees of marginalized groups to expand their networking and visibility opportunities. If your firm does not have a diverse staff and/or diverse leadership, exposure to a larger pool of professionals could increase these employees' odds of connecting with someone who can advise them from a similar lived experience. Such an opportunity could, in turn, connect them with other diverse talent to potentially refer to your firm, creating a new pipeline you may not have accessed otherwise.

Crowdsource Increasing Cultural Competence

Ask your staff what's important to them. Lead a firmwide activity like a design sprint to surface ideas directly from your staff about how they think your organization can increase in cultural competence. The results can be astounding when a workforce is given a voice to influence the ways an organization works, primarily because they are more intimately familiar with the challenges of executing the work than the leaders who are often called upon to strategize. And because the majority of diversity often exists among the ranks of organizations, as opposed to leadership, establishing culturally competent practices is going to require an adjustment to the assumption about where true expertise really lies.

Empower Your Employee Resource Groups (ERGs)

Invite your ERGs or internal affinity groups to weigh in on corporate strategic discussions. Don't just tap them to host cultural observances or town halls following a tragedy in the headlines. Include them in planning sessions to provide input for recruiting strategies, retention efforts, and business development tactics. Inquire about trends and patterns they're seeing both internally and externally that could help your organization stay ahead of the game from a cultural standpoint. Show them that they are not just window dressing and that you value their firsthand experiences, which are representative of increasingly growing segments of our society, your future talent pool, and your expanding customer base.

Revolutionize Your Practice to Set the Tone for Your Industry

Are you prepared to blaze new paths in your industry? Here are some ideas to expand your influence beyond your four walls and challenge your profession to step up in meaningful ways.

Utilize Industry Associations as a Platform

Use your voice through platforms like industry associations. Use your clout as a sponsor or partner organization to force change. Push for event topics and communities of practice that promote cultural competence. Negotiate the details of your sponsorship to support such efforts. Team up with other industry leaders to demand more topic and speaker diversity at conferences and events. Identify and endorse speakers of different backgrounds for conferences and keynotes. Only sponsor or participate if there is an agreement on the composition of the speaker panel.

Team Up with Minority-Owned Design Firms

Approach minority-owned design firms and invite them to share the stage with you at industry events. Invite them to co-sponsor industry activities and ensure there are equitable opportunities for exposure and promotion. Share their stories among your circles. Familiarize yourself with their work, so you can speak confidently to their reputation and expertise when potential business development opportunities arise.

Connect with Networks of Designers of Diverse Backgrounds

It is not uncommon for designers of diverse backgrounds to seek out professional organizations and activities beyond their workplace to expand their network and find the support, mentors, and connections they don't get through work. Therefore, designers of diverse backgrounds are likely connected to affinity organizations that would never show up on your radar, offering them everything from professional networking to mentoring and community service opportunities to apply their skills. Take time to get to know the designers in your firm and what networks they're a part of. Inquire about whether and how your firm could provide needed resources to support the mission of those networks. Consider offering to sponsor or host activities in your workspace. Lend your social capital and connect them to contacts that could boost the organization's visibility or access to donors.

Revolutionize Design Education by Sharing Your Knowledge

As keepers of the insights of "others," we as designers of diverse backgrounds possess extremely valuable knowledge. I'm confident that we are bold enough to make space for and insert our truth into the design dialogue.

As designers, part of what we do is bring ourselves to our work and embed our own flavor into what we create. We have to incorporate our identity into our work to truly make it ours. That's what makes it designed rather than manufactured. Is our cultural identity not part of our fingerprint? We have to fight to keep it from being edited out. If we get edited out, so do those who identify like us.

Design students: Boldly incorporate elements of your identity into your work. Push back when your design choices are challenged by peers or instructors. If enough students commit to this practice, it will become the norm.

Design professionals: Take your talents and knowledge back to the classroom — this time in the front of the room. Be the professor you wish you had. Be the mentor who encourages students to imprint their culture on their work. Be the faculty member who pushes colleagues to adjust their grading criteria, syllabi, and speaker panels by setting an example in your own course. Be the leader who pushes for reform from inside the system, challenging department heads to incorporate concepts like design justice into their programs.

Revolutionize Design in Your Own Individual Way

Chances are that your experience in design has brought challenges or inequities to your attention that are not even mentioned in this book. I invite you to take up an issue that ignites a spark in you — one that fires you up every time you think about it — and commit to doing something about it. I have two personal interests that I'd like to champion. One is exposing young children of color to careers in design, so we can build a solid, diverse pipeline of future designers. I had the advantage of being raised by a mother educated in design, which put design on my radar as a viable career path. But that's not everyone's reality, especially people raised in cultures that view more traditional careers in law, medicine, and business as more prestigious and stable. My hope is that reaching children of diverse backgrounds from an early age could help expand their horizons and possibly even those of their families and communities.

Another interest of mine is intentionally promoting design as a profession to people of varied abilities and mental health backgrounds. Nothing fosters more empathy and creativity in a designer than lived experience. Too often, our default is to just bring in people of certain identities for focus groups or product tests. If they were trained as designers themselves, their perspectives could be baked into the design process from the very beginning. I'd be willing to bet that their increased presence would also go a long way in prompting the mindset, environment, and behavior shifts necessary to revolutionize our industry.

We as designers have an enormous task ahead of us to ensure that our professions mirror and keep up with the realities of our evolving world. We must meet that task with the requisite passion, commitment, and intensity if we're going to move the mark. This book has spelled out the opportunities to make an impact, from asking simple questions in a team meeting to ways to shake up entire industries. In the next chapter, we'll reflect on where and how you can get started.

 Scan this QR code to download a **discussion guide** for this chapter.

7
TAKE
ACTION

Design is expression. Design is creativity. Design is a service. Design is an act. As designers, action is what we do. As culturally competent designers, change is the action that's required. Consider the following points in making your own plan to become a culturally competent designer.

Your Individual Plan

As a design student or designer, take time to reflect on your own design practices and the ones presented in this book.

1. Think about how you have or have not treated cultural identity in your own design practice. What factors have enhanced or limited your awareness of the importance of cultural identity in design?

2. What can you do to evolve your own culturally competent design practices? Review the six habits of culturally competent designers (Chapter 3) and the Design for Identity Blueprint (Chapter 5). Select at least one activity you can start now and set one goal you would like to achieve over the next six to twelve months.

3. Write a statement declaring what you would like your legacy to be as a designer. Reflect on the concepts in this book and others that may be personal to you in terms of cultural identity. Think about how you will use your influence to incorporate cultural competence into the dialogue in the spaces you inhabit as a designer.

Your Design Firm's Plan

As a design firm leader or owner, you have the power and influence to make cultural competence a priority in your organization. Equipped with the six habits of culturally competent designers (Chapter 3), insights into what it will take to make the shift to a culturally competent organization (Chapter 4), the Design for Identity Blueprint for the culturally competent design process (Chapter 5), the aspirational vision of design as activism (Chapter 6), and the interest that likely drew you to this book in the first place, you can start from right where you are.

1. From an organizational standpoint, think about how you have or have not treated cultural identity in your firm's design process and practices. What factors have enhanced or limited your awareness of the importance of cultural identity in design?

2. Revisit your firm's mission, vision, and values and identify whether and how the values of diversity, equity, inclusion, and belonging resonate with who you are. Evaluate in what ways those values could be extended to the services you provide to customers.

3. Assess your organization's current mindset, behaviors, and environment as they relate to cultural competence, cultural identity, difference, diversity, equity, inclusion, and belonging. Evaluate these factors internally as a workplace and externally as a service provider. Remember: Consistency among your staff and in interactions with clients and customers is critical to your brand (Chapter 1). In what ways could you stand to grow as an organization?

4. Decide what you are prepared to do as a design firm to increase your cultural competence. Think about what resources (time, money, labor) you're willing to commit and within what timeframe. Determine how this effort aligns with your strategic vision. If necessary, restate that vision to reflect the priority you place on culturally competent design.

5. Consider how you will communicate your culturally competent design stance to your employees, job seekers, and current and future clients and customers. The intentionality and authenticity of this step will go a long way in establishing your commitment.

6. Strategize about how you will get your staff on board and cement culturally competent design practices into your way of being as a firm. How will you make these practices outlast you, inspire adoption, and continue to evolve as the organization evolves?

BOOST YOUR CULTURE QUOTIENT

You don't want to just wing it when it comes to formally adopting a culturally competent design stance and implementing the practices this requires. Whether it's someone internal or external to your organization, be sure to consult with a DEIB expert to formulate a plan for structuring and managing this transformation, measuring progress, and making it stick. Their knowledge will be invaluable in terms of providing relevant guidance, especially regarding communication.

The words in this book are meaningless if they inspire only thought and not action. The ultimate hope is that they will bring about a shift that spans design disciplines and brings about impactful outcomes for people who have been marginalized, dismissed, and erased from the design dialogue. Make a commitment to do your part to begin reversing the harm that's been done. Each of us has a part to play in making design inclusive in impactful ways, and we can all start right now.

Scan this QR code to download the **Individual Plan** worksheet and the **Design Firm Plan** worksheet.

AFTERWORD

by Kia Weatherspoon

Is this profession for me?"

This was a question asked by one of my Black, heterosexual, former military, male students with his hair in individual twists in the fall of 2022. I had to vehemently and intentionally look him in his eyes and say, "Yes! There is space for you in this industry." This student also has a background in IT.

While my response was strong and firm, it still pained me because I knew this moment was atypical. The odds of a straight Black male student in an interior design program feeling okay to express that level of comfort or vulnerability with a middle-aged white woman are one in a million. Now, this is where I'm "supposed" to insert some data on the demographic makeup of educators in design programs, which I will not do because we often use data to absolve us of the obvious injustice that exists right in front of us.

Instead, I'll say as a nationally recognized speaker and award winning licensed interior designer who has spoken at over thirty schools over the past decade, I can count on one hand the number of times I've encountered professors of color. If I want to be more specific and call out a Black professor, I can sadly say it's one or two.

Which is why for me data has always been the prime example of what's keeping us from seeing what empathy can solve right now. Our focus should be understanding that the experiences of people of color are more valid, human, and empathetic than any datapoint. Our stories are trusted resources for change. But the stories have to be told, acknowledged, and reflected upon.

Story 1

Me: Tell me how to say your name again?

Me: Two more incorrect pronunciations.

Student: Just call me Laura.

Me: NO! I will not call you the whitest of white girl names. Help me again, please. I've never spoken Chinese, so it will take me some time. But I'm going to get it right.

Two days later I accidentally shared my screen while I had YouTube videos up of how to pronounce the student's name.

As a person of color, I had a deficit or a moment of ignorance. Yes, ignorance. A word which has become derogatory or an insult. But if you look at the literal definition it means lacking knowledge or information. However, as a person of color first and professor second, what was more important than my comfortability or embarrassment of getting it wrong twice would have been to reinforce this student had/has to whitewash her identity for the comfort of others. Literally the apparent thing that identifies her cultural heritage, her name, she was so willing to relinquish. To be clear there was no fault in her action. It stemmed from an understanding that academia mirrors the professions it's training people for. Our profession, like many, is still, and for many years to come, will be predominantly white.

As a person of color, I have heard countless stories of this notion of code switching, assimilating, and conforming. This is something I have never done! (I will come back to that.) As an educator, but more importantly as a human being, we all have to be staunch in our efforts and our resolve to teach students to show up as they are in the simplest of ways. It requires our collective effort to stop whitewashing space and our profession. This means starting to teach students and professors to unlearn behaviors — behaviors so common as changing their name to ease how others addressed them. It is unacceptable.

Story 2 (*This story is paraphrased for context and anonymity.)

"I have been coming to this industry event for a number of years. Obviously, after the racial unrest I have gotten more recognition, even though I've been in this industry for years. Franklin* has literally exploded onto the scene of this event in the past year, and his face is literally on the first three pages. I had to talk to him about the optics immediately because I see what the event organizers are doing." - Michael*

Michael is a 6'3", dark skin Black male. He looks more like a football player than interior designer.

Franklin is a mixed raced, but obviously Black, light-skinned male who strategically presents as gay.

What are "they" doing? This now fosters the notion of colorism, where a fair-skinned person of color is much more acceptable or approachable than a dark-skinned one. It's how gay male designers are celebrated and revered as the taste makers. These narratives have persisted in, if not saturated, our industry since its inception, characterizing who interior design is meant for as a craft and profession.

This story also made me reflect on the number of LatinX and Hispanic designers who openly express their white facing appearance is safer to lead with than their cultural heritage. Or Asian designers who express their safety in white spaces because they are seen as a more docile or "safe" minority. Our industry will pit us against each other if we do not openly address these injustices head on.

Story 3

"Your work doesn't look like affordable housing. It looks like a luxury condo project!"

I have heard many variations of this perceived "compliment" when people talk about the work Determined by Design does. I have heard it from real estate developers, governmental agencies, architects, and other interior designers. The latter of that group often perplexes me. My face gives me away first before I quizzically ask, "What is affordable housing 'supposed' to look like?"

I've garnered many responses but the crux of the question is just fucking flawed!

The U.S. Department of Urban Housing has a definition of affordable housing. However, the stripped-down version is housing for people of a lower socio-economic status. At times affordable housing was referred to as Section 8, subsidized housing, ghetto, or a more recently adopted term "work-force housing."

This abridged contextual definition was necessary. Because as interior designers, our job is to design for ALL people. Not just those in the "luxury" project type. For an interior designer to even question a building type that didn't look appropriate for a specific group of people reflects how far we have to go as a profession.

We have to stop asking, "Who is interior design for?" Instead, we need to think about how we design elevated spaces for everyone. How do we design interior spaces where everyone's cultural and historical narrative are reflected? When do we stop allowing trends to dictate the spaces we create for others? I want to pause here as it's critical...

Earlier I mentioned the whitewashing of spaces. There has been a consistent removal of color from products ranging from furniture to accessories to textiles. Literally, while recently walking numerous showrooms with the new product introduction all I saw was beige, cream, and white natural textiles, furniture, accessories. You look in industry magazines from hotels, retail, and homes. You see these beige, light wood tones, and creams winning all the awards. And I don't have enough time to talk about the color gray!

This matters because the removal of color from interior spaces is also...

A removal of culture.

A removal of heritage.

It perpetuates that there is no place for vibrancy.

It's reinforcing that individualism is not celebrated.

Which leads us to a critical question: If the spaces we design as interior designers have to be whitewashed and neutral, how do/can I as a professional or educator show up as myself? How do I design for those who don't look like me? How do I teach those who have a different background than me?

It starts with empathy.

It's fostered by listening.

It enacts change when you bring others to the table.

It's relinquishing what you know and always searching for understanding.

It's educating on why. "Why?" is the most important question an interior designer can ask, repeatedly.

It's rooted in searching for context and history, not trends.

It's understanding that designing based on your personal style is ego, but design based on the story of the people is Design Equity™.

It's searching for and celebrating the individual identities of those often seen as the minority.

Creating space for others is to embrace them fully as they are. To embrace others through design you must first learn to embrace your full identity. I have attributed much of my success in this industry to three key things:

1. I have always shown up as my whole self. Even when I was "the only" in the room. Showing up as just Kia was enough.

2. I lead/design with empathy. If the space is not good enough for my loved ones, then it's not good enough for anyone else's.

3. I don't want an identifiable design style. I want to narrate the stories of others through color, textures, designed elements, and art.

What I strive for the most is for the stories I've shared here to become narratives of the past. Where young Asian Pacific students don't alter their identity for comfort, colorism doesn't attempt to pit us all in place of disadvantage, and no one will ever question again "Is this a profession for me?"

As you reflect on this book, remember we are charged with the craft of creating space for all people. We are in service to families and communities because the design decisions we make now will affect four generations of families.

How will you make space for everyone?

Kia Weatherspoon

CID, NCIDQ, ASID, D.F.A (h.c), Founder + President, Determined by Design

ACKNOWLEDGMENTS

To the amazing and diverse group of individuals who contributed your perspectives and experiences to this book — I'm so grateful to have crossed paths with all of you at various points in my career. You all add something special not only to these pages but to your respective fields.

To Candice L. Davis, my book coach who I also consider myself fortunate to call a friend — it was no coincidence that you were a part of this journey with me. I felt your investment in seeing this through with me and for me. I can't thank you enough.

To the designers and DEIB practitioners I've had the pleasure to collaborate with and learn from in my work — thank you for giving me hope that the ideas in this book could actually take root and influence the future direction of our professions.

To the talented, supportive women who made my cover photo shoot happen – thank you for making it a day to remember. Much respect to Delores Holloway of a little bit of whimsy photography, hairstylist Melanie Holliway, and makeup artist Flo Carey of Blend Blot Blush. You all are the best!

To my mother, who vicariously experiences all of my highest highs and my lowest lows, both personally and professionally – thank you for loving me as only you can. Whenever someone was mean to me as a child or tried to make me feel bad about myself, I would think, "Well, if God and Mom love me, I can't be that bad." You lifted me up then and you still lift me up now. I'm grateful to be your daughter.

To my family — I wouldn't be me without you. You are my foundation. You gave me everything, including my unshakeable faith. Thank you for supporting me along my unconventional career path and cheering me on mostly because you knew I was too stubborn to be convinced otherwise. Lol! Who would have known all those first chapters of mystery books that I started writing in grade school and my Sweet Stuff, Inc. greeting cards would lead to this?! (Hold onto them — they could be collector's items one day! Ha!) I love you all more than I can say, and I thank God for you every day. I do this work in honor of the generations who came before me and the ones who will come after.

To my UVA crew — you are the greatest gift I took away from my undergrad experience. Who would have thought when I arrived in Charlottesville that I would leave years later with an extended lifelong family? And just like family, you've cheered me on all along the way. I love and appreciate each of you so much.

To my dear friends and to my Sorors of Zeta Phi Beta Sorority, Incorporated (especially the Tau Theta and Nu Xi Zeta chapters) — you all add so much to my life. You have seen me through so many seasons, challenges, highs, and lows. Thank you for being my village and for always having confidence in me.

To my colleagues-turned-friends and my professional connections-turned-friends — I am so thankful that our paths aligned in these many different ways. You all bring something so special and unique to my life, and it wouldn't be the same without a single one of you. Support and encouragement from your family and inner circle is one thing, but receiving it from people who have absolutely no obligation to do it is something completely different. Thank you for your belief in me and challenging me and telling me I would do big things even when neither of us knew exactly what that would look like.

To the Philadelphia public schools that shaped me and the teachers who inspired me and guided me in my most formative years, both academically and artistically:

James R. Lowell School — the place where the seeds for my career in Diversity, Equity, Inclusion, and Belonging were planted back in the early 80s. I had the great fortune to begin school in an environment with people from so many racial, ethnic, religious, and other backgrounds, and all I knew was they were my classmates and friends. There was magic there that I took for granted until I grew up and encountered so many people who had grown up having limited interaction with people who were different from themselves. My experiences there make their way into many conversations I have up to this very day. Those years weren't without controversy or challenges, but the outcomes were life-changing in some of the most uplifting ways. Thank you, Mrs. Sherman, Mrs. Kramer, Mrs. Ezekiel, Mrs. Eisner, Mrs. Smith, Mrs. Cooper, and Ms. Taylor.

Julia R. Masterman Laboratory and Demonstration School — another place of great growth, exposure, and learning, partially in the classroom and partially from taking the Broad Street line to and from school starting at age ten! I still remember standing on the stage giving a speech at the eighth grade graduation and staring at the banner that said "Dare to be excellent." Those words and that challenge definitely stuck. Thank you, Mrs. Levine, Mrs. Winokur, and Mr. Oxley.

Central High School — proud to represent 253, the best to ever do it! And proud to be a part of a family legacy of Central students. So many life lessons, so many opportunities, and so much support to push myself and strive for things I hadn't realized were within my reach. Thank you, Mr. Cutler, Mr. Byrd, Mrs. Weston, Mr. Perry, Mr. Huber, and Mrs. Maimon.

APPENDIX

ADDITIONAL RESOURCES TO BOOST YOUR CULTURE QUOTIENT

The following is a list of resources you will find helpful in your practice as a culturally competent designer. This list is by no means exhaustive, but it's a great place to start.

Toolkits & Guides

- ▶ The American Institute of Architects (AIA) Guides for Equitable Practice (https://www.aia.org/resources/6246433-guides-for-equitable-practice)

- ▶ Microsoft Inclusive Design Toolkits (https://www.microsoft.com/design/inclusive/)

- ▶ Design Studio First Aid Kit by Lily Song and Allentza Michel (CoDesign at GSD) (https://research.gsd.harvard.edu/cdli/files/2020/06/CoDesignFirstAidKit_Zine-3.pdf)

- ▶ Anti-Racism Design Resources List (Design as Protest Collective) (https://www.dapcollective.com/resources)

- ▶ Anti-Racist Design Justice Index (Design as Protest Collective) (https://www.dapcollective.com/index)

- ▶ IBM Racial Equity in Design - Advancing Racial Equity in Design: A Field Guide for Managers and Leaders (https://www.ibm.com/design/racial-equity-in-design/the-work/field-guide/)

- ▶ Design Ethically Toolkit by Katherine M. Zhou (https://www.designethically.com/toolkit)

Research

- ▶ Inclusive Design and the Black Experience (Gensler) - https://www.gensler.com/gri/inclusive-design-and-the-black-experience?q=inclusive%20 design%20process

- ▶ Design Equity through Policy Action (Gensler) - https://www.gensler.com/gri/ design-equity-through-policy-action

Podcasts

- ▶ *Breaking the Silence of Design*

- ▶ *It's About Time* (IBM Racial Equity in Design)

- ▶ *The Design of Business | The Business of Design*

Books

- ▶ *Design Justice: Community-Led Practices to Build the Worlds We Need* by Sasha Constanza-Chock

- ▶ *Design for the Other 90%* by Barbara Bloemink and Cynthia E. Smith

- ▶ *Designing for Growth* by Jeanne Lidtka and Tim Ogilvie

- ▶ *Extra Bold: A Feminist, Inclusive, Anti-Racist, Non-Binary Field Guide for Graphic Designers* by Ellen Lupton, Farah Kafei, Jennifer Tobias, Josh A. Halstead, Kaleena Sales, Leslie Xia, and Valentina Vergara

- ▶ *Invisible Women: Data Bias in a World Designed for Men* by Caroline Criado Perez

- ▶ *Reimagining Design: Unlocking Strategic Innovation* by Kevin Bethune

Organizations

- ▶ African American Graphic Designers
  (https://aagd.co/)
- ▶ Dark Matter University
  (https://www.darkmatteruniversity.org)
- ▶ Design as Protest Collective
  (https://www.dapcollective.com/)

Schools/Programs

- ▶ Pensole Lewis College of Business & Design
  (https://pensolelewiscollege.com/)
- ▶ Baltimore Design School
  (https://baltimoredesignschool.com/)
- ▶ Rural Studio - School of Architecture, Planning
  and Landscape Architecture of Auburn University
  (http://ruralstudio.org/)

Professional Development

- ▶ IIDA Academy Collective D(esign) Webinar Series
  (https://iida.org/academy)
- ▶ IIDA Talent Collective
  (https://iida.org/talent-collective)

Blog

- ▶ Start Where You Are
  (https://www.jessicabantom.com/startwhereyouare)

Thought Leaders & Pioneers

- ► June Ambrose, Creative Director, Costume Designer, and Entrepreneur

- ► Ruth E. Carter, Academy-Award Winning Costume Designer

- ► D'Wayne Edwards, Founder and President of Pensole Lewis College of Business & Design

- ► Jason Mayden, Designer, Educator, Entrepreneur, Author of *A Kids Book About Design*

 Scan this QR code to download a **listing of the resources** in this appendix.

ABOUT THE AUTHOR

Jessica Bantom is a Diversity, Equity, Inclusion & Belonging (DEIB) practitioner and workplace strategist who helps develop customized strategies for organizations that bring about transformational change. A compelling speaker, certified facilitator, and coach, Bantom seeks to enable people and organizations to reach their full potential and actualize the values of inclusion and belonging no matter what position they hold. Jessica is also active in the interior design industry as an interior design and color consultant and as a DEIB champion committed to promoting meaningful change in the profession.

Bantom's career is informed by her ongoing dedication to exploring the intersection of design and diversity. Jessica completed her master's degree in Interior Design at Marymount University in Arlington, Virginia, and obtained her bachelor's degree at the University of Virginia in Charlottesville, where she also completed a specialization in Design Thinking and Innovation from Darden Executive Education. At Georgetown University, Jessica received credentials as a Change Management Advanced Practitioner (CMAP), and she is certified as an Associate Diversity Coach through the CoachDiversity Institute in collaboration with the Howard University School of Business. She holds a certificate in Diversity and Inclusion from Cornell University.

In addition, Jessica is certified by Veritas Culture as a Culture Facilitator and Diversity & Belonging Facilitator, and is also a Certified Change Management Professional (CCMP) and Prosci Certified Change Practitioner.

A proud member of Zeta Phi Beta Sorority, Incorporated, Jessica is a long-time resident of the Washington DC area, although she will always call Philadelphia home.

CPSIA information can be obtained
at www.ICGtesting.com
Printed in the USA
JSHW071605100523
41522JS00001B/1